MW01622865

From My Travels to Your Table

NORMA JEAN WILL, M.D.

A COLLECTION OF RECIPES TO DINE FOR

From My Travels to Your Table

Published by Norma Jean Will, M.D.

Cover design by Paul van den Berg
Food photography by Gregory Hindahl, M.D.

This cookbook is a collection of favorite recipes,
which are not necessarily original recipes.

ISBN: 978-0-9801792-0-0
SAN: 855-417X

Edited, Designed, and Manufactured by
CommunityClassics™

An imprint of

FRP™

P. O. Box 305142
Nashville, Tennessee 37230
800-358-0560

Manufactured in the United States of America
First Printing: 2008
3,000 copies

Dedication

This book is dedicated to my fiancé, best friend, and soul mate, Gregory Hindahl. I can't wait to spend the rest of my life with you!

The time to eat is now in season;
Dust in the kitchen, there's just no reason.

Appetizers, entrées, desserts, and much more;
There's enough for everyone, so keep an open door.

God is great, and God is good,
The world is just one big neighborhood.

So gather friends and family, and share how you feel;
By the end of the stay, you'll have a five "thumbs-up" meal!

–Kaylyn Hindahl

Table of Contents

Acknowledgments

I am forever indebted to my ultimate best friend, Gregory Hindahl, for his endless support and encouragement throughout this project. His exquisite photography, editing, and taste-testing skills are greatly appreciated and second to none. A special thanks to Paul van den Berg for the phenomenal cover design at a "discount design" price! You are such an awesome friend! A special thank-you also to Mr. Ben Vereen for allowing me to use his photograph and tell our Jamaican baked oatmeal story. Thanks also to Jerrilee Lamar and Lee Ann Blue for allowing me to use their photograph and tell their story.

A great big hug and heartfelt thanks to my family as follows for their endless love, support, and volunteer taste-testing: my parents, Barbara and Leroy Will; my sisters Judy Peckenpaugh, Joyce Will, and Nancy Burden; and my brother John Will. Thanks to Danielle and Vern Germano, lifelong friends, with whom I have cooked and shared many fine meals and good times over the years. A warm fuzzy thanks to Clay Angel for being the kind of best friend I could borrow money from, loan money to, live with, share a car with, and never share a cross word with (OK, unless you're messing up stuff in my kitchen!). A "bear hug" thanks to Laura Rogers for being the kind of best friend that will do anything CRAZY! I wouldn't have nearly as many stories to tell if it weren't for you. Because of you, I also have stories that I will never tell—only take to my grave! Thanks to Vito Rocco, "The Kid," for always raving about my cooking and for introducing me to Italian cuisine. Thanks to Chris Aghayan and Teny Haroutunian for teaching me about Armenian cuisine. Thanks to Vincent Tang and Lonnie Nguyen for supplying sushi-grade salmon and teaching me about Vietnamese cuisine. Thanks to Marion and Theunis van den Berg for introducing me to South African cuisine. Thanks to Sangeeta Dhara for welcoming me into her home and introducing me to oysters and Tasmanian/Indian cuisine!

Thanks to the staff at Deaconess Medical Group-West (Carrie Owen, Thelma Pruitt, Rebecca Glover, Joan Jenkins, Mindi Pretzsch, and Rebecca Ray) for your constant willingness to sample new recipes and offer opinions—with the usual opinion being: I need to bring more food into the office!

Thanks to Kaylyn Hindahl for taking time away from geometry proofs to write a poem for this book! Thanks to Kiersten Hindahl for not only sampling the recipes but actually "eating" the cookbook cover. Thanks to Cortney Hindahl for flying all the way to California with us to confirm that the Tuscan Bean Dip recipe truly is "to DINE for."

Introduction

So what do going to medical school, riding a camel in the Sahara Desert, and snorkeling the Great Barrier Reef have to do with food? These are only a few of my life experiences that have had a major influence on my cooking and have inspired many of my recipes.

At age twenty-eight, I found myself newly divorced and alone but with a bachelor's degree in biology. What was I going to do? Well, go to medical school, of course! But did I want to study medicine in Indiana? Heck no! I had always wanted to live abroad, so . . . why not go to medical school abroad and kill two birds with one stone? That was how my travel obsession started, and it hasn't stopped. Some of the places I visited during my studies include ten of the Caribbean islands, England, Scotland, France, Germany, Belgium, the Netherlands, Tunisia, Spain, Italy, South Africa, Australia, New Zealand, and Tasmania. I was constantly inspired to broaden my cooking skills during and after visiting these magnificent places. All of these experiences ignited and fueled my desire to create recipes from all over the world. The culinary adventures resulting from my travels have been almost endless. I look forward to sharing some of these with you in this cookbook. I have included many stories relating my recipes to the adventures that inspired them. Some are quite comical, and I hope you find them as entertaining as others do.

While many of my recipes were inspired by dishes I've had abroad, some are simply concoctions I've created. I warn my friends and family when serving them a new creation. I always say, "This tastes really good in my head." Luckily I haven't had many flops, and everyone is excited when these recipes find their way from my head to their plates. Some of these recipes were created in my head at 3 a.m. after getting paged while being on call. I have horrible insomnia, which is often related to getting calls from patients all night long. Once I'm awake, I can't stop thinking. I've turned this occupational hazard into a positive thing by keeping a notebook by the bed and creating new recipes in the middle of the night. If my pager won't let me sleep, I figure I might as well get something done.

My traveling didn't stop when I graduated from medical school. During residency I had the opportunity to go on a mission trip to Jamaica. The hospital where I did a residency in family medicine has a sister hospital in Annotto Bay, Jamaica. Annotto Bay is part of St. Mary Parish and is considered the poorest area of Jamaica. Staff from our hospital visit the area once or twice a year to provide medical care in area clinics. These "clinics," usually schools or churches, are located in rather remote areas up in the mountains of Jamaica.

The people attending these clinics would likely not receive medical care if it weren't for our organization providing support in the form of doctors, nurses, pharmacists, and free medications. Many of the Jamaicans have severe diabetes or high blood pressure and no way to get treatment. During each trip we try to give each patient a two- to three-month supply of medicine for diabetes, high blood pressure, or in many cases, both.

It is amazing that some of the Jamaicans in the clinics have never seen the ocean. Yet they live on an island and, in some cases, are only five miles from the coast! This is due to a lack of transportation, treacherous washed-out roads, and the lack of simple necessities such as shoes. With the first mission trip, I was hooked. Missionary medicine is extremely rewarding. The patients arrive at the clinic at 8 a.m. and wait all day just to see a doctor. They are so appreciative that they go all out in preparing lunches and drinks for us. Curried goat is always a staple. Even though it's quite yummy, I didn't include a recipe for it, since I've never been able to get fresh goat in any of our local grocery stores. Nor did I include a recipe for their goat head soup! You don't even want to know what you can find floating on the top of that soup!

As a physician, I am concerned about the health and well-being of not only my patients but also the patrons of this cookbook. I have to admit, some of these recipes are quite rich, but I believe all things should be enjoyed in moderation. So be sure to exercise, get plenty of sleep, and take good care of yourself!

I hope you enjoy the stories. I also hope you enjoy cooking and serving these dishes as much as I enjoyed creating them. That's enough chatting—let's get cooking!

Visa/Visas

Vietnamese Egg Rolls

Nigiri Sushi

Crab-Stuffed Mushrooms

Dolmas

Rumaki

Stuffed Grilled Eggplant

Prosciutto-Wrapped Scallops

Spicy Mayonnaise

Citrus Soy Dipping Sauce

Lemon Pepper Fried Oysters

Yin Yang Shrimp

Calamari with Sweet Thai Chili Sauce

Spicy Sesame Chicken Wings

Tuscan Bean Dip

Spinach and Artichoke Dip

Jerk Chicken Wings

Great Starters

Chinese Caribbean Sushi and Vietnamese Alaskan Egg Rolls?

The first time I had sushi was at the Kontiki Beach Bar on Orient Beach in St. Maarten. My friend Anna was visiting from Indiana. Luckily for me, it was during a time of reprieve from intense studying, so I could actually go to the beach with her. We had been swimming, snorkeling, and lying out on the beach all day and we were starving. We checked out the beach bar restaurants scattered along the shore. The Kontiki Hut intrigued us with its sushi menu. I had never eaten sushi and neither had Anna. "What the heck!" she said. "Let's try it."

We had no idea what we were ordering. When it arrived, it looked really interesting, especially the ones with orange fish eggs on top. We learned later that those fish eggs are called salmon roe. I was so hungry by the time it arrived, I would have eaten an ostrich egg! Some people are afraid to try sushi, but we weren't. We tore into it. It was like nothing I had ever eaten before. I was definitely a sushi lover. Now I had to figure out how to make the stuff. My favorite was the salmon nigiri sushi. But where could I get sushi-grade salmon and not pay an arm and a leg for it? Anna returned to Indiana, but I could not stop thinking about how I wanted that sushi again.

One advantage of living and studying abroad is getting to meet people from all over the world. One of my classmates, Vinny, was Chinese and lived in Orange County, California, before starting medical school. Lonnie, his fiancée, was Vietnamese and lived in Alaska with their adorable three-year-old daughter. She had decided to stay in Alaska with her family while Vinny completed his first two years of medical school in St. Maarten. Vinny went to Alaska at every break to see his fiancée and daughter. Coincidentally, Lonnie's two brothers were professional fishermen in Alaska. Hmmmm.

I wondered if they fished for salmon in Alaska. Turns out they caught tons of salmon, so all I had to do was ask and Vinny brought me free fresh salmon iced down in a cooler.

I found a "how-to" sushi kit at the local grocery store, and even though I had never made sushi before, I love new challenges. I studied the book and the ingredients and tackled the sushi challenge head on! Before I knew it, I was cranking out nigiri sushi, California rolls, and temaki, or hand rolls.

After the first year, our classes were still hard, but we got better at learning massive amounts of material. This gave us a little more time to enjoy the island. Second year was when Lonnie decided to move to St. Maarten to be with Vinny. She brought their daughter Crystal with her. I was always cooking for some get-together or another, including on holidays and for visiting family. One day Lonnie wanted to put on a dinner and show us how to entertain Vietnamese-style. It was awesome. She made a shrimp dish, stir-fried rice, and vegetables. But my favorite was her Vietnamese egg rolls. I watched her make them but failed to get the recipe from her. I caught up with her in Alaska a few years later while I was on vacation. Her brothers were still fishing, and she insisted on packing up a cooler of fresh salmon for me to take home. This time I didn't even have to ask for the salmon, but I again forgot to get the egg roll recipe. Eight years after I first saw them made, I re-created the egg rolls from the depths of my memory. They were even better than I remembered. They are so flavorful you don't even need dipping sauce. I haven't seen Lonnie in years, but if she ever sees this cookbook, I hope she likes my egg rolls as much as I liked hers!

Vietnamese Egg Rolls

Filling
1 1/2 pounds extra-lean ground pork
1 carrot, grated
2 garlic cloves, crushed
2 scallions, chopped
1/4 cup water chestnuts, chopped
1/2 teaspoon finely grated fresh ginger
1 tablespoon oyster sauce
1 tablespoon soy sauce
1 teaspoon sesame oil
1/4 teaspoon freshly ground pepper
1/4 teaspoon salt

Rolls
12 to 14 egg roll wrappers
1 egg
1 tablespoon water
Peanut oil for frying

For the filling, combine the pork, carrot, garlic, scallions, water chestnuts, ginger, oyster sauce, soy sauce, sesame oil, pepper and salt in a large bowl and mix well.

For the rolls, place an egg roll wrapper on a work surface with one point facing you. Beat the egg with the water in a small bowl. Brush the mixture over the edges of the wrapper. Spoon 2 to 3 tablespoons of the filling 2 inches from the bottom corner of the wrapper. Fold the bottom point over to within 1/2 inch of the opposite point, forming a triangle. Fold the two outside points to the center so they just meet. Roll up snugly from the center toward the remaining point. Press lightly to seal. Repeat with the remaining egg roll wrappers and filling.

Heat enough peanut oil to cover the egg rolls to 325 degrees in a deep skillet or other deep pan. Fry six egg rolls at a time for 18 to 20 minutes or until the pork is cooked through and the wrappers are medium brown. Remove the egg rolls and drain on paper towels. Serve immediately or keep warm in a 250-degree oven until serving time.

Makes 12 to 14 egg rolls

Nigiri Sushi

2 cups short grain sushi rice
2 cups plus 2 tablespoons water
1/4 cup rice vinegar
2 tablespoons sugar
1 teaspoon salt
1 teaspoon wasabi paste
6 ounces sushi-grade salmon or tuna, cut into 1/4- to 1/2-inch bite-size pieces

Rinse the rice in cold water two or three times until the water drains clear. Drain the rice in a colander for 30 minutes. Combine the rice and the water in a medium saucepan with a tight-fitting lid. Bring to a boil. Reduce the heat and simmer, covered, for 15 to 20 minutes or until the liquid is absorbed. Remove from the heat and let steam, covered, for 15 minutes longer. Combine the vinegar, sugar and salt in a small saucepan. Cook over medium heat until the sugar and salt dissolve. Combine the rice and the vinegar mixture in a wooden bowl. Toss lightly with a wooden spoon. Let stand until cool. (You may use a fan to speed up the process.)

Wet your hands and pick up 2 tablespoons of the rice. Cup it in your palm to form a log. Press your opposite index finger down the middle of the roll to firmly pack the rice. Spread a thin layer of wasabi paste down the length of the roll. Place on a serving plate and top with a piece of the fish. Repeat with the remaining rice, wasabi paste and fish. Serve immediately.

Makes 4 servings

Crab-Stuffed Mushrooms

1 pound mushrooms
2 tablespoons butter
2 teaspoons minced shallot
2 garlic cloves, minced
8 ounces cream cheese, softened
1/2 cup mayonnaise
2 (6-ounce) cans lump crab meat
1/4 cup bread crumbs
1/2 cup (2 ounces) grated Parmesan cheese
2 tablespoons chopped pimento
2 tablespoons chopped parsley
Dash of hot red pepper sauce
Salt and pepper to taste

Preheat the oven to 400 degrees. Remove the stems from the mushrooms and finely chop the stems, reserving the mushroom caps. Heat the butter in a skillet. Add the mushroom stems and sauté for 2 minutes. Add the shallot and garlic and sauté until tender. Combine the mushroom mixture, cream cheese and mayonnaise in a bowl and mix well. Add the crab meat, bread crumbs, Parmesan cheese, pimento, parsley, hot sauce, salt and pepper and mix well. Scoop about 1 tablespoon of the mixture into each mushroom cap, rounding and smoothing the mixture as you turn the mushroom cap. Bake in a shallow baking dish for 25 to 30 minutes or until the mushrooms are tender and the stuffing is golden brown.

Makes 4 servings

Dolmas

2 tablespoons olive oil
1 small onion, chopped
2 garlic cloves, minced
1 pound ground lamb
3/4 cup long grain rice
1 1/2 cups chicken broth
2 tablespoons mint, chopped
2 tablespoons parsley, chopped
Salt and pepper to taste
2 tablespoons pine nuts, toasted and chopped
2 tablespoons lemon juice
8 ounces grape leaves in brine
2 tablespoons olive oil
Juice of 1 lemon

Heat 2 tablespoons olive oil in a large skillet over medium heat. Add the onion and garlic and sauté until tender. Add the lamb and cook until brown, stirring until crumbly. Add the rice and cook for 1 minute. Add the broth, mint, parsley, salt and pepper and cook until the liquid is absorbed. Remove from the heat and stir in the pine nuts and 2 tablespoons lemon juice. Let stand until cool.

Remove the grape leaves from the brine; rinse the grape leaves and pat dry. Place 1 to 2 tablespoons of the lamb mixture in the center of each leaf. Fold both sides of the leaf in toward the center. Roll tightly to enclose the filling. Repeat with the remaining grape leaves and lamb mixture, reserving several leaves to line the bottom of a large skillet. Arrange the stuffed grape leaves in a double layer in the skillet. Add 1 inch of water to the skillet. Drizzle 2 tablespoons olive oil and the juice of 1 lemon over the grape leaves. Place over medium-high heat and bring the water to a boil. Reduce the heat and simmer, covered, for 20 to 30 minutes. Serve warm or cold. Drizzle with additional olive oil and lemon juice, if desired.

Makes 6 servings

Rumaki

1 pound chicken livers
16 slices bacon, cut into halves

Sauce
2 tablespoons butter
1 shallot, minced
2 garlic cloves, crushed
1/2 cup ketchup
1/4 cup soy sauce
1/4 cup packed dark brown sugar
2 tablespoons rice wine vinegar
1 teaspoon chili sauce
Freshly ground pepper to taste

Preheat the grill to 375 degrees. Wrap one chicken liver in one piece of the bacon and secure with a wooden pick. Repeat with the remaining chicken livers and bacon.

For the sauce, melt the butter in a small skillet. Add the shallot and garlic and sauté until brown. Stir in the ketchup, soy sauce, brown sugar, vinegar, chili sauce and pepper. Simmer for 15 to 20 minutes. Arrange the bacon-wrapped chicken livers in a single layer in a grill basket. Grill for 25 to 30 minutes or until the bacon is evenly crisp, turning once or twice. Baste frequently with the sauce during the last 10 minutes.

Makes 6 servings

Stuffed Grilled Eggplant

2 Japanese eggplant
Salt to taste
2 garlic cloves, crushed
1/4 cup olive oil
2 tablespoons fresh thyme, finely chopped
Freshly cracked pepper to taste
4 to 6 ounces goat cheese

Preheat the grill to 350 degrees. Cut the stem off each eggplant and cut each eggplant lengthwise into 1/4-inch slices. Sprinkle with salt and place in a colander to drain for 30 minutes; pat dry. Mix the garlic with the olive oil in a small bowl. Brush the mixture over the eggplant slices. Season with thyme and pepper. Grill for 15 to 20 minutes, turning once. Let stand until slightly cooled. Place 1/2 ounce (about 1/2 tablespoon) of the goat cheese at one end of each eggplant slice and roll tightly to enclose. Drizzle with additional olive oil, if desired.

Makes 6 servings

Prosciutto-Wrapped Scallops

1 pound medium scallops
4 ounces prosciutto
1/2 cup Italian salad dressing
2 tablespoons fresh parsley, chopped

Preheat the broiler to 500 degrees. Wrap each scallop with a slice of prosciutto and secure with a wooden pick. Combine the scallops with the salad dressing in a sealable plastic bag. Seal the bag and marinate for 10 to 15 minutes; drain. Arrange the scallops in a single layer on a nonstick baking sheet. Broil for 2 to 3 minutes on each side or until the scallops are golden brown. (If you prefer, thread the scallops onto a skewer and grill them.) Serve immediately.

Makes 4 servings

Spicy Mayonnaise

1/4 cup mayonnaise
1 to 2 teaspoons Sriracha chile sauce

Combine the mayonnaise and chile sauce in a small bowl until well blended. Spoon into a small squeeze bottle and drizzle back and forth over sushi.

Makes 1/4 cup

Citrus Soy Dipping Sauce

1/4 cup soy sauce
1/4 cup orange juice
1/4 cup fresh lemon juice
2 tablespoons seasoned rice vinegar

Combine the soy sauce, orange juice, lemon juice and vinegar in a small bowl and mix well.

Makes about 1 cup

Lemon Pepper Fried Oysters

Oysters
12 to 14 large oysters, shucked
Lemon pepper marinade
1 1/2 cups all-purpose flour
1 teaspoon salt
1/2 teaspoon pepper
Vegetable oil for frying

Dipping Sauce
1/2 cup mayonnaise
2 tablespoons grated horseradish
2 tablespoons spicy brown mustard
1/4 cup honey

For the oysters, marinate the oysters in the marinade for 30 minutes. Combine the flour, salt and pepper in a sealable plastic bag. Drain the oysters, discarding the marinade. Add the oysters to the bag and seal tightly. Toss to coat well. Heat the oil in a deep skillet over medium-high heat. Shake any excess flour mixture from the oysters. Fry the oysters in the oil for 3 to 4 minutes on each side or until golden brown, turning once; drain.

For the dipping sauce, combine the mayonnaise, horseradish, mustard and honey in a small bowl and mix well. Serve the oysters with the dipping sauce.

Makes 4 servings

Yin Yang Shrimp

Shrimp
Peanut oil for frying
3/4 cup all-purpose flour
1/4 cup cornstarch
1 teaspoon salt
1/2 teaspoon pepper
2 eggs
2 tablespoons milk
2 pounds fresh or thawed shrimp,
peeled, deveined and tails removed

Sauce
5 ounces cream of coconut
1/2 cup mayonnaise
2 to 4 tablespoons garlic chili sauce
(adjust to desired heat level)
Lettuce
Chopped fresh scallions

For the shrimp, heat the peanut oil to 400 degrees in a deep fryer. Preheat the oven to 450 degrees. Combine the flour, cornstarch, salt and pepper in a large sealable plastic bag. Beat the eggs with the milk in a bowl. Dip the shrimp into the egg mixture, and then coat with the flour mixture. Shake off any excess flour. Fry for 4 to 6 minutes or until the coating is golden brown; drain.

For the sauce, whisk the cream of coconut, mayonnaise and chili sauce in a medium bowl until well blended. Arrange the shrimp in a 9×13-inch baking dish. Pour the sauce over the shrimp. Bake for 12 to 15 minutes, stirring every 4 to 5 minutes to distribute the sauce evenly. Serve over a bed of lettuce and top with scallions.

Makes 6 to 8 servings

Note
For a shortcut, use frozen precooked batter-dipped shrimp.

Yin Yang Shrimp–The "Noncoconut" Coconut Shrimp

I named this dish Yin Yang Shrimp because of the opposite but harmonious combination of the sweet and spicy flavors. I love coconut shrimp, as does my family. But my sister Joyce does not like the texture of coconut, although she loves the flavor (some people are weird like that!). I figured I could get around this if I used cream of coconut in the sauce but left the coconut flakes out of the breading. The first time I made this for my family, we were all in Arkansas visiting my brother John. The shrimp smells incredible as it bakes, and family members were all hovering around the kitchen, anxiously waiting for the shrimp to come out of the oven. As soon as my father tasted it, he demanded to know how long I had known about this recipe (afraid he had missed out on previous servings). I assured him I had only made it up a couple of weeks prior. He made sure my mother got the recipe before the end of the day. It is now a frequently requested dish at our family get-togethers.

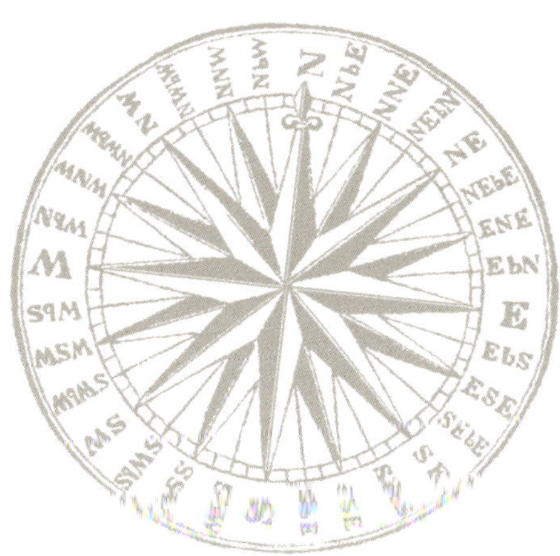

Calamari with Sweet Thai Chili Sauce

Canola oil for frying
1 cup all-purpose flour
1/2 teaspoon salt
1/4 teaspoon pepper
1 pound squid tubes, cut into 1-inch rings
2 eggs
2 tablespoons milk
6 ounces panko
2 garlic cloves, mashed to a paste
1/2 cup mayonnaise
Sweet Thai chili sauce

Heat the canola oil to 375 degrees in a deep fryer. Combine the flour, salt and pepper in a sealable plastic bag. Add the squid and toss to coat well. Remove the squid and shake off any excess flour. Beat the eggs with the milk in a medium bowl. Spread the panko in a shallow dish. Dip the squid into the egg mixture and then roll in the panko. Deep-fry for 2 minutes or until the coating is golden brown; drain. Combine the garlic with the mayonnaise in a bowl and mix well. Serve the calamari with the chili sauce and the garlic mayonnaise.

Makes 4 servings

Spicy Sesame Chicken Wings

Chicken
Vegetable oil for frying
2 cups all-purpose flour
Salt and pepper to taste
2 eggs
2 tablespoons milk
2 pounds chicken wings

Sauce
1/2 cup soy sauce
1/2 cup water
2 tablespoons sherry or bourbon
1/4 cup white vinegar
1 1/2 cups sugar
2 teaspoons sesame oil
1 tablespoon garlic chili paste

For the chicken, pour enough oil into a large skillet or electric skillet to come halfway up the side of the skillet. Heat the oil to 350 degrees. Combine the flour, salt and pepper in a large sealable plastic bag. Beat the eggs with the milk. Dip the chicken wings in the egg mixture and place them one at a time in the flour mixture. Seal the bag and shake to coat well. Shake off any excess flour. Fry in the hot oil for 20 to 24 minutes or until the coating is golden brown and the chicken is cooked through, turning to cook evenly; drain on paper towels. Arrange the wings in a 9×13-inch baking dish.

For the sauce, preheat the oven to 400 degrees. Combine the soy sauce, water, sherry, vinegar, sugar, sesame oil and garlic chili paste in a medium saucepan. Bring to a boil. Reduce the heat and simmer for 20 minutes.

Pour the sauce over the chicken. Bake for 20 minutes, turning three or four times to coat the chicken evenly. Remove to a serving platter. Garnish with a sprinkling of sesame seeds.

Makes 6 servings

Note
For a shortcut, use breaded frozen chicken breast strips.

Tuscan Bean Dip

8 ounces mascarpone cheese, softened
1/2 cup olive tapenade
1 (15-ounce) can cannellini beans, drained and rinsed
1 tablespoon olive oil
2 Roma tomatoes, finely chopped
2 tablespoons pesto
8 ounces shredded Italian-blend cheese

Preheat the oven to 350 degrees. Spread the mascarpone cheese evenly over the bottom of a 9×9-inch baking dish. Top with the olive tapenade, spreading evenly. Combine the cannellini beans and olive oil in a food processor; process until smooth. Spread over the tapenade. Toss the tomatoes and pesto in a bowl. Spread over the bean layer. Sprinkle the Italian-blend cheese evenly over the top. Bake for 20 to 25 minutes or until the cheese is melted. Serve with pita chips or crostini.

Makes 6 servings

Spinach and Artichoke Dip

12 ounces frozen chopped spinach, thawed and drained
8 ounces cream cheese, softened
1/2 cup mayonnaise
1 (10-ounce) jar marinated artichoke hearts, drained and coarsely chopped
2 garlic cloves, minced
1/2 cup (2 ounces) grated Parmesan cheese
Salt and pepper to taste

Preheat the oven to 350 degrees. Press out the excess moisture from the spinach. Combine the cream cheese, mayonnaise, spinach, artichoke hearts, garlic, Parmesan cheese, salt and pepper in a bowl and mix well. Spoon into a large au gratin baking dish. Bake for 20 minutes. Serve with pita chips or corn chips.

Makes 6 servings

Jerk Chicken Wings

1/2 cup chopped onion
3 garlic cloves, minced
1 Scotch bonnet chile or jalapeño chile, seeded and chopped
2 tablespoons dark brown sugar
2 tablespoons soy sauce
2 tablespoons dark rum
2 tablespoons vegetable oil
1 tablespoon fresh lime juice
1 tablespoon fresh thyme, chopped
1 teaspoon lime zest
1 1/2 teaspoons ground allspice
1 teaspoon freshly ground pepper
1/4 teaspoon cinnamon
1/8 teaspoon freshly ground nutmeg
2 pounds chicken wings

Combine the onion, garlic, chile, brown sugar, soy sauce, rum, oil, lime juice, thyme, lime zest, allspice, pepper, cinnamon and nutmeg in a food processor. Pulse until mixed. Place the chicken wings in a large sealable plastic bag. Pour the spice mixture into the bag and seal. Shake to coat well. Marinate in the refrigerator for 4 to 10 hours. Preheat a grill to medium-hot. Remove the chicken from the marinade, discarding the marinade. Grill in a grill basket for 30 to 40 minutes or until the juices run clear when the chicken is pierced with a fork.

Makes 6 servings

Note
This marinade also works well for pork and for fish steaks.

Coconut Curry Pumpkin Soup

Creamy Chicken Noodle Soup

Lobster Bisque

Monterey-Blend Mushroom Soup

French Onion Soup

Hearty Split Pea Soup

Seafood Chowder

Mojito Avocado Salad

Coronation Chicken Salad

Oriental Chicken Salad with Peanut Dressing

Spinach Salad with Warm Goat Cheese

Red, White and Bleu Salad

Winter Salad with
Blue Cheese and Walnut Balsamic Vinaigrette

Mediterranean Salad

Soups & Salads

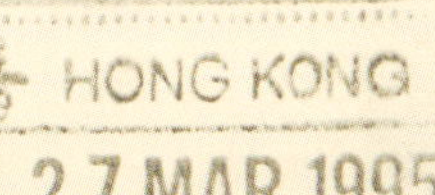

Curry Pumpkin Soup and Jerk Chicken Wings

One of my very favorite adventures was my first mission trip to Jamaica. Since coming to Deaconess Hospital, I have been on three Jamaican mission trips. My duties at work include teaching family medicine residents, and I hope to go on many more mission trips and show "my" residents what an awesome experience it is. It means a lot to me that the hospital I work for supports such an important program.

We get very attached to the people we meet and treat at Jamaica's Annotto Bay Hospital and the area clinics. I can't help but want to keep going back to do whatever I can to help them. The local hospitality always begins with a friendly reception the night of our arrival. We are greeted with a cup of warm curried pumpkin soup, a welcome treat because we stay by the sea, where nights can be cool.

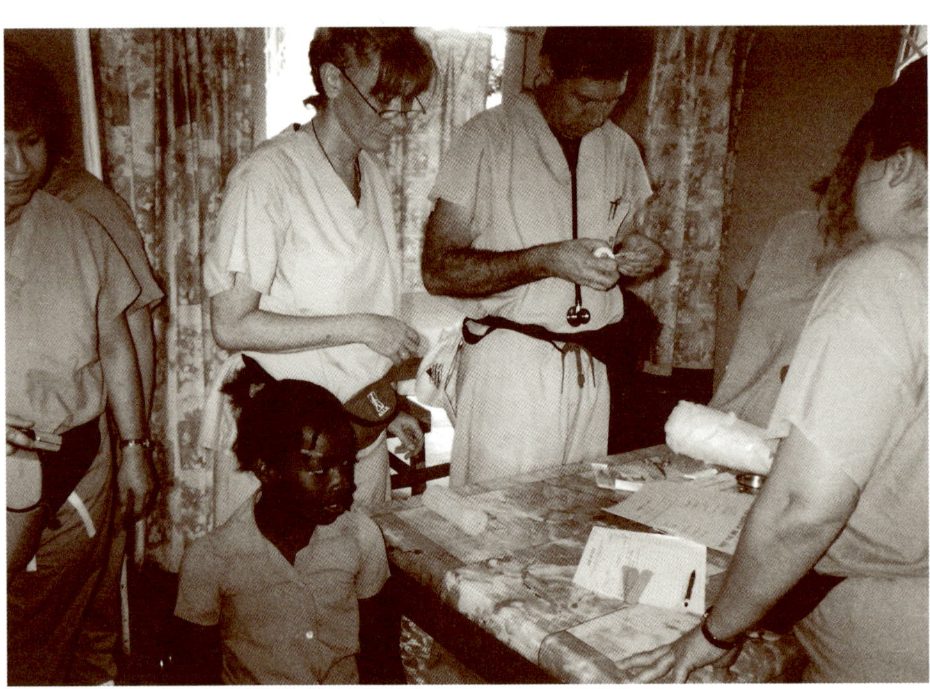

Each day a team of ten to twelve clinical staff makes its way up the rugged roads through the mountains of Jamaica to treat people in these remote areas. Our goal is to arrive by 9 a.m., and when we arrive, there are usually between 120 and 200 people waiting to see us. We see patients of all ages, from newborns to pregnant women to centenarians. While we are setting up our medical equipment and medications, the locals socialize and cook our lunch. On one particular day we had a lovely meal of jerk chicken, beans and rice, and fresh tropical fruit. We ate quickly and returned to work. It was time for school to dismiss, bringing kids for a checkup or treatment.

That day, a ten-year-old girl came in limping. One look at her foot and I could tell it was broken. We did not have any casting supplies, so I was at a loss. I told her family they really should go to the hospital in Annotto Bay. The grandmother began crying, saying they had no ride to the hospital and no money to pay. I asked my attending physician, Dr. Hindahl, if he had any ideas. By this time, both the girl and the grandmother were crying. She was scared, but we assured her we would take care of her. We rummaged through our supplies and found a solution: we made a splint for her foot out of wooden tongue depressors. We taped them together like a raft and padded them with gauze and an ACE wrap. Once it was on her foot, the now-smiling Jamaican girl said it felt much better. She showed us she was able to walk without pain. We explained that she needed to take it easy and use the splint for the next few weeks to give her foot a chance to heal. We didn't want her walking all the way home on her broken foot, so we loaded her up in our van and took her home. She must have felt better by then because she got to the bottom step of the van and jumped off, landing squarely on both feet. Again we emphasized the "taking it easy" part, but she was one tough little girl.

We realized then how many people in this part of Jamaica lacked good-soled shoes. On a subsequent trip, we took boxes of hundreds of pairs of shoes donated by the employees of our hospital. They were a big hit with patients. That was a couple of years ago, but I still see patients wearing some of "our" shoes. It really warms the heart to know you are touching peoples' lives and giving some comfort, even if it is as simple as a pair of shoes!

Coconut Curry Pumpkin Soup

2 tablespoons butter
1 small onion, chopped
2 garlic cloves, crushed
1 tablespoon curry powder
2 teaspoons ground coriander
1/2 teaspoon ground cumin
1/2 teaspoon white pepper
2 chicken bouillon cubes
1 1/2 cups warm water
2 (15-ounce) cans pumpkin
1 (14-ounce) can coconut milk
2 tablespoons dark brown sugar
1 cup heavy cream
Salt and pepper to taste

Melt the butter in a medium stockpot. Add the onion and garlic and sauté until tender. Add the curry powder, coriander, cumin and white pepper and mix well. Sauté briefly to release the flavors. Dissolve the bouillon cubes in the water. Add the bouillon, pumpkin, coconut milk and brown sugar to the stockpot and mix well. Bring to a boil. Reduce the heat and simmer for 20 to 30 minutes. Remove from the heat and let stand to cool slightly. Purée the soup in a blender or food processor until smooth. Pour through a fine strainer. Return the soup to the stockpot. Bring to a boil. Reduce the heat and add the cream. Season with salt and pepper and mix well. Serve garnished with a dollop of sour cream or crème fraîche and chives.

Makes 6 servings

Creamy Chicken Noodle Soup

6 tablespoons butter
1/2 large sweet onion, chopped
2 ribs celery, chopped
1 large carrot, chopped
1/4 cup all-purpose flour
5 cups milk
3 chicken bouillon cubes
2 cups hot water
10 ounces wide egg noodles
2 cups chopped roasted chicken

Melt the butter in a large nonstick stockpot over medium heat. Add the onion, celery and carrot and sauté until tender. Stir in the flour and cook for 1 minute. Add the milk and mix well. Dissolve the bouillon cubes in the water and add to the soup. Bring to a simmer, stirring frequently. Add the noodles and chicken. Cook for 15 to 18 minutes or until the noodles are tender.

Makes 6 servings

Lobster Bisque

6 tablespoons butter
2 carrots, finely chopped
1 rib celery, finely chopped
2 shallots, minced
2 garlic cloves, minced
6 tablespoons all-purpose flour
1 (6-ounce) can tomato paste
1/4 cup Cognac
4 cups fish stock
1 cup white wine
2 sprigs of tarragon
1 sprig of thyme
2 sprigs of parsley
1 bay leaf
Dash of hot red pepper sauce
Pinch of freshly grated nutmeg
Salt and freshly cracked pepper to taste
1 1/2 cups heavy cream
12 ounces lobster tail meat, sliced

Melt the butter in a stockpot over medium heat. Add the carrots, celery, shallots and garlic and sauté until tender. Stir in the flour. Add the tomato paste and cook for 1 minute. Stir in the brandy and stock. Add the wine. Make a bouquet garni by tying together the tarragon, thyme, parsley and bay leaf. Add the bouquet garni, hot sauce, nutmeg, salt and pepper to the soup and mix well. Bring to a boil. Reduce the heat to low and simmer for 30 minutes. Remove the bouquet garni. Pour the soup into a blender or food processor and process until smooth. Pour through a strainer or chinois. Return the soup to stockpot and stir in the cream. Heat through. Ladle into individual soup bowls and top with the lobster. Garnish with crème fraîche and chives.

Makes 6 servings

Monterey-Blend Mushroom Soup

1 (1-ounce) package Monterey-blend dried mushrooms
1/2 cup white wine
2 tablespoons butter
2 teaspoons minced shallot
1 garlic clove, minced
8 ounces button mushrooms, finely chopped
1 tablespoon all-purpose flour
1 1/2 cups heavy cream
1/4 teaspoon white pepper
Salt to taste

Combine the Monterey-blend mushrooms and wine in a 1-quart saucepan. Bring to a boil over high heat. Remove from the heat immediately and set aside. Melt the butter in a 2-quart saucepan. Add the shallot and garlic and sauté until tender. Add the button mushrooms and sauté until tender. Sprinkle the flour over the button mushrooms and stir until moistened. Add the cream and cook until thickened and bubbly, stirring constantly. Add the Monterey-blend mushrooms and any remaining wine. Season with the pepper and salt. Ladle into soup bowls and garnish with chopped chives.

Makes 4 servings

French Onion Soup

1/4 cup (1/2 stick) butter
3 large sweet onions, sliced
2 garlic cloves, minced
2 tablespoons all-purpose flour
4 cups beef broth
1/2 cup sherry or white wine
1 teaspoon Worcestershire sauce
2 sprigs of fresh thyme
2 sprigs of fresh parsley
1 bay leaf
1 teaspoon salt
1/2 teaspoon freshly cracked pepper
8 (1-inch-thick) slices French bread
Olive oil
Garlic cloves
8 ounces Gruyère cheese, shredded

Melt the butter in a stockpot. Add the onions and sauté until tender and almost caramelized. Add 2 garlic cloves and sauté until the garlic is tender and the onions are caramelized. Add the flour and mix well. Cook for 1 minute. Add the broth, sherry and Worcestershire sauce and mix well. Tie the thyme, parsley and bay leaf together in a bouquet garni. Season with salt and pepper and bring to a boil. Reduce the heat and simmer for 30 minutes. Remove the soup from the heat and discard the bouquet garni. Preheat the oven to 450 degrees. Brush the bread with olive oil and rub with additional garlic cloves. Bake until golden brown. Ladle the soup into four soup crocks or ovenproof serving bowls. Float two slices of the bread on top of each bowl of soup. Top each with 2 ounces of the cheese. Bake the soup until the cheese is melted, bubbly and golden brown. Watch carefully because the cheese may burn quickly. Let stand to cool for 15 minutes.

Makes 4 servings

Hearty Split Pea Soup

2 tablespoons butter
1 onion, chopped
2 celery ribs, chopped
2 carrots, chopped
8 cups water
1 ham bone
2 cups dried split peas, rinsed and sorted
1 bay leaf
2 sprigs of thyme
2 sprigs of parsley
Salt and pepper to taste

Melt the butter in a large stockpot. Add the onion, celery and carrots and sauté until tender. Add the water and ham bone and bring to a boil. Add the peas. Tie the bay leaf, thyme and parsley into a bouquet garni and add to the soup. Reduce the heat and simmer, covered, for 2½ to 3 hours or until the peas are soft. Remove the ham bone. Let the soup stand until cool. Remove the bouquet garni. Pour the soup into a blender or food processor and process until smooth. Return to the stockpot. Cut the meat from the ham bone and dice or shred. Return the ham to the soup. Season with salt and pepper.

Makes 6 servings

"Heavenly" Split Pea Soup

As a poor medical student living on a rather pricey island, I loved getting visitors. Getting visits meant getting loot from home. Everyone knows you are allowed to check two bags on a flight. At that time, you were permitted two 70-pound bags. Any time one of my sisters or friends came to visit, they knew they could only pack one suitcase for themselves, because the other was for me! Mom made sure to pack it with my favorite cooking ingredients, and she usually included a few treats as a surprise. Did I mention I'm the baby of the family and very spoiled?

Don't get me wrong, you can get world-class cuisine on the island of St. Maarten. However, when milk costs $8 per gallon and you're living on student loans, you look forward to the free stuff. As time went on, my mother got more and more creative with her packing techniques. I happened to mention to her that I didn't have a microwave. Next thing you know, my sister Joyce came to visit. I noticed she was hauling not just a suitcase but a huge cooler as well. I asked what was in the cooler, and she just smiled and said, "You'll have to wait until we get to your apartment. It's a surprise."

Back at my apartment, I opened the cooler and couldn't believe my eyes. Mom and Joyce had figured out how to send a microwave from Indiana to the Caribbean—in a cooler. But that's not all. Not only did they have goodies stuffed around the outside of the microwave, but when I opened the microwave, there was a huge frozen Heavenly Ham inside. I had hit the jackpot!

All week my friends, my sister, and I pigged out (no pun intended). But that wasn't the end of it. My sister made sure to get a ham with a bone in it, and Mom had also sent split peas. So after my sister left, I made up a big pot of split pea soup. Boy, did that hit the spot. My friends said it was the best split pea soup they had ever had. It sure helped me get over my post-family-visit funk. My sister Judy was the next to visit, and I'll be darned if she didn't bring a ham and split peas, too. From then it became a tradition and a very good one at that!

Seafood Chowder

6 tablespoons butter
1 onion, finely chopped
2 ribs celery, finely chopped
1 large carrot, chopped
1/4 cup all-purpose flour
4 cups milk
1 pound potatoes, peeled and finely chopped
1 sprig of thyme
1 spring of parsley
1 bay leaf
2 cups heavy cream
2 pounds mixed seafood (whole baby clams, oysters, lump crab meat, calamari, shrimp)
Salt and pepper to taste

Melt the butter in a stockpot over medium heat. Add the onion, celery and carrot and sauté until tender. Add the flour and stir to mix. Add the milk and cook until the soup boils, stirring constantly. Add the potatoes. Tie together the thyme, parsley and bay leaf into a bouquet garni and add to the soup. Reduce the heat and simmer, covered, until the potatoes are al dente. Add the cream and seafood and mix well. Simmer for 15 to 20 minutes longer. Remove the bouquet garni. Season with salt and pepper.

Makes 6 servings

Mojito Avocado Salad

1 ripe avocado
1 Granny Smith apple, chopped
8 to 10 cherry tomatoes, cut into halves
1 tablepoon finely chopped fresh mint
Juice of 1 lime
2 tablespoons sour cream

Reserve one-fourth of the avocado for the dressing. Chop the remaining avocado into bite-size pieces. Combine with the apple, tomatoes, mint and lime juice in a medium bowl and mix well. Mash the reserved avocado until creamy. Combine with the sour cream in a bowl and mix well. Spoon the dressing over the salad and stir gently. Garnish with fresh mint and a lime. Serve immediately.

Makes 4 servings

Coronation Chicken Salad

1/2 cup mayonnaise
1/4 cup honey
2 teaspoons curry powder
1/4 teaspoon garlic powder
Salt to taste
2 cups cubed cooked chicken
1/2 cup chopped mango
1/4 cup golden raisins
1/2 cup slivered almonds

Combine the mayonnaise, honey, curry powder, garlic powder and salt in a medium bowl and mix well. Add the chicken, mango, raisins and almonds and toss to coat. Serve on croissants, pita slices, wraps, whole wheat bread or buttery crackers.

Makes 4 servings

Oriental Chicken Salad with Peanut Dressing

Peanut Dressing
1/3 cup creamy peanut butter
1/4 cup peanut oil
2 tablespoons soy sauce
2 tablespoons rice wine vinegar
2 tablespoons sherry
2 tablespoons dark brown sugar
1 tablespoon chili sauce
2 teaspoons sesame oil

Salad
1 head napa cabbage, shredded
2 grilled large chicken breasts, cut into slices
1 large carrot, grated
4 ounces fresh bean sprouts
1/2 cup snow peas, cut into bite-size pieces
1 (8-ounce) can sliced water chestnuts, drained
1/4 cup fresh cilantro, chopped
1/4 cup roasted peanuts, chopped
1/2 cup crunchy rice noodles or crumbled dry ramen noodles

For the dressing, combine the peanut butter, peanut oil, soy sauce, vinegar, sherry, brown sugar, chili sauce and sesame oil in a bowl and whisk to blend.

For the salad, combine the cabbage, chicken, carrot, bean sprouts, snow peas, water chestnuts and cilantro in a large bowl. Pour the dressing over the salad and toss to coat. Top with the peanuts and rice noodles and garnish with additional cilantro.

Makes 6 servings

Spinach Salad with Warm Goat Cheese

Sweet-and-Sour Dressing
8 slices bacon
1 tablespoon minced shallot
1 tablespoon all-purpose flour
1 cup cran-raspberry juice
2 tablespoons white vinegar
3 tablespoons honey
1 tablespoon Dijon mustard
Salt and freshly ground pepper to taste

Salad and Assembly
2 tablespoons butter
8 slices herbed goat cheese
1 egg, beaten
1/2 cup dry bread crumbs
1 large package washed fresh spinach
2 hard-cooked eggs, finely chopped
1/4 cup dried cranberries
1/4 cup sliced almonds
1 pint fresh raspberries

For the dressing, cook the bacon in a skillet until crisp and brown; drain, reserving 2 tablespoons of the drippings in the skillet. Crumble the bacon and set aside. Add the shallot to the skillet and cook until tender. Add the flour and cook for 1 minute, stirring constantly. Add the cran-raspberry juice and vinegar. Cook until thick and bubbly, stirring constantly. Add the honey and Dijon mustard. Cook until well blended and bubbly, stirring constantly. Season with salt and pepper. Set aside.

For the salad, melt the butter in a skillet over medium-high heat. Dip the cheese into the egg and coat with the bread crumbs. Fry the cheese for 20 to 30 seconds on each side. Divide the spinach among four salad plates. Top with the eggs, cranberries, almonds, raspberries and bacon. Drizzle with the warm dressing. Top each salad with two slices of the fried cheese.

Makes 4 servings

Red, White and Bleu Salad

Raspberry Vinaigrette
1/4 cup raspberries, crushed and pressed through a sieve
1 teaspoon minced shallot
1/4 cup raspberry blush vinegar
2 tablespoons simple syrup or honey
1 tablespoon Dijon mustard
1/4 cup canola oil
1 tablespoon fresh parsley, finely chopped
Salt and freshly cracked pepper to taste

Salad
4 cups spring lettuce mix
1/2 cup sliced strawberries
1/2 cup fresh blueberries
4 ounces bleu cheese, crumbled
1/3 cup pistachios

For the vinaigrette, combine the crushed raspberries, shallot, vinegar, simple syrup and Dijon mustard in a small bowl and whisk to mix well. Add the canola oil in a fine stream, whisking constantly until emulsified. Stir in the parsley, salt and pepper.

For the salad, combine the lettuce, strawberries, blueberries, cheese and pistachios in a large bowl. Pour the vinaigrette over the salad and toss to coat.

Makes 4 servings

Winter Salad with Blue Cheese and Walnut Balsamic Vinaigrette

Walnut Balsamic Vinaigrette
2 tablespoons balsamic vinegar
1 teaspoon minced shallot
1 teaspoon Dijon mustard
2 tablespoons honey or corn syrup
1 tablespoon walnut oil
1/4 cup olive oil
2 tablespoons finely crumbled blue cheese
1 teaspoon fresh parsley, minced

Salad
1 small onion, sliced
Olive oil for sautéing
4 cups spring lettuce mix
1 red pear, thinly sliced
1/4 cup walnuts, coarsely chopped
4 ounces blue cheese, crumbled

For the vinaigrette, combine the vinegar, shallot, Dijon mustard, honey and walnut oil in a bowl and whisk to blend. Add the olive oil in a fine stream, whisking constantly until emulsified. Add the cheese and parsley and mix well.

For the salad, sauté the onion in olive oil in a skillet until the onion is caramelized. Let stand to cool. Layer the lettuce, pear, onion, walnuts and cheese on salad plates. Drizzle with the vinaigrette.

Makes 4 servings

Mediterranean Salad

Lemon Herb Dressing
1/4 cup lemon juice
1 tablespoon sugar
1 teaspoon minced shallot
2 garlic cloves, minced
2 teaspoons fresh oregano, finely chopped
2 teaspoons fresh mint, finely chopped
1/2 cup extra-virgin olive oil
2 tablespoons minced black olives
2 tablespoons feta cheese, finely crumbled
Salt and freshly cracked pepper to taste

Salad
1 large head romaine, chopped
1 small cucumber, peeled and chopped
4 ounces artichoke hearts, chopped
1/2 cup grape tomatoes
1/2 cup kalamata olives
1 small yellow bell pepper, chopped
4 ounces feta cheese, crumbled
1 small red onion, sliced (optional)
1 cup garlic croutons

For the dressing, combine the lemon juice and sugar in a small bowl, whisking to dissolve the sugar. Add the shallot, garlic, oregano and mint and mix well. Add the olive oil in a fine stream, whisking constantly until emulsified. Stir in the olives and cheese. Season with salt and pepper.

For the salad, combine the lettuce, cucumber, artichoke hearts, tomatoes, olives, bell pepper, cheese and onion in a medium bowl. Pour the dressing over the salad and toss to coat. Top with the croutons and serve immediately.

Makes 6 servings

Visa/Visas

Crab Eggs Benedict

Spanish Quiche

Jamaican Baked Oatmeal

Domies

Berry-Stuffed French Toast

Tall Buttery Biscuits with Gravy

Cajun Breakfast Potatoes

Roast Chicken, Red Pepper and Havarti Pitas

Shrimp Scampi and Bacon Pizza on the Grill

Croque Monsieur

Duck Breast Sandwiches

King of Club Sandwiches

Italian Steak Panini

Oyster Po' Boys

Breakfast & Lunch

Crab Eggs Benedict

Eggs Benedict
2 English muffins, split into halves
4 slices Canadian bacon, crisp-cooked
8 ounces lump crab meat
(Dungeness or blue crab)
4 tablespoons milk
4 eggs

Blender Hollandaise Sauce
4 egg yolks
Dash of salt
Dash of cayenne pepper
1/2 cup (1 stick) butter
Juice of 1/2 lemon

For the eggs Benedict, preheat the oven to 200 degrees. Butter the cut side of the English muffins. Toast buttered side down in a skillet. Place buttered side up in a baking dish. Top each muffin half with a slice of Canadian bacon. Arrange 2 ounces of the crab meat on each muffin half. Place in the oven to keep warm. Spray four 1/2-cup ramekins with nonstick cooking spray. Spoon 1 tablespoon of the milk into each ramekin. Break one egg into each of the ramekins. Microwave the ramekins individually for two 15- to 20-second intervals or until the egg white is set but the yolk is not. Remove with a slotted spoon and place on top of the English muffins.

For the hollandaise sauce, combine the egg yolks, salt and cayenne pepper in a blender or food processor and process until smooth and thick. Heat the butter in a small saucepan until it melts and begins to bubble. Remove from the heat. Pour the hot butter and then the lemon juice into the blender, processing constantly until smooth. Spoon warm hollandaise sauce over each serving of eggs.

Makes 2 servings

Note
If you are concerned about using raw or barely cooked eggs, use eggs pasteurized in their shells, which are available at some specialty food stores, or use an equivalent amount of pasteurized egg substitute.

Spanish Quiche

1/2 cup chorizo
1 cup (4 ounces) shredded Manchego cheese
1 unbaked frozen (9-inch) deep-dish piecrust
1/4 cup chopped sun-dried tomatoes
1 tablespoon chopped fresh chives
1 (10-ounce) can cream of mushroom soup
3 eggs, beaten
1/4 cup milk
1 teaspoon chopped fresh oregano
1/4 teaspoon Spanish sweet paprika
4 to 6 strands of saffron
Freshly ground pepper to taste

Preheat the oven to 400 degrees. Brown the chorizo in a skillet, stirring until crumbly; drain. Sprinkle the cheese evenly over the bottom of the piecrust. Layer the chorizo, tomatoes and chives over the cheese. Beat the soup, eggs, milk, oregano, paprika, saffron and pepper in a bowl. Pour over the layers and smooth the top. Cover the edge of the piecrust with foil. Bake for 30 minutes or until the crust is golden brown and the center of the quiche is set. Let cool for 15 to 20 minutes before slicing.

Makes 6 to 8 servings

Jamaican Baked Oatmeal

1/2 cup (1 stick) butter, softened
3/4 cup packed brown sugar
3 eggs
1/2 cup cream of coconut
1 cup milk
1 teaspoon vanilla extract
3 cups quick-cooking oats
2 teaspoons baking powder
1/2 teaspoon baking soda
1/2 teaspoon salt
3 bananas, mashed
1/2 cup chopped fresh pineapple, or 8 ounces canned crushed pineapple, drained
1/2 cup flaked coconut
1/4 cup pecans, chopped

Preheat the oven to 350 degrees. Cream the butter and brown sugar in a large bowl. Add the eggs one at a time and mix well. Add the cream of coconut, milk and vanilla and mix well. Set aside. Combine the oats, baking powder, baking soda and salt in a bowl. Add the oat mixture to the butter mixture. Fold in the bananas, pineapple, coconut and pecans. Spread evenly in a greased 9×13-inch baking dish. Cover with foil and bake for 20 minutes. Uncover and bake for 15 to 20 minutes longer or until the top is golden brown.

Makes 8 servings

The Good Friday Jamaican Baked Oatmeal

My fiancé and food photographer, Greg, is a family physician and is the medical coordinator for our hospital's mission trips to Jamaica. This episode occurred on a trip made by our mission group in the spring of 2005. I wasn't able to go on the trip, but the incident inspired my recipe for Jamaican Baked Oatmeal.

Our group was returning from Jamaica to Atlanta. Our vice president of nursing, Lee Ann, and our director of employee education, Jerrilee, were sitting next to a middle-aged man, and Greg was sitting across the aisle from them. The middle-aged man was working with the flight attendant to secure a seat in the front of the plane near his very young daughter. Just before the plane left the gate, the gentleman returned to his assigned seat and asked Lee Ann and Jerrilee if they would mind if he traded seats with Ben Vereen. They thought he was joking until Mr. Vereen walked down the aisle and asked if they minded his sitting next to them. They could hardly speak!

As they introduced themselves, Mr. Vereen mentioned that he lives in Jamaica part-time and asked about their visit. They explained their medical mission work in Annotto Bay. He thanked them for coming to help "his" people. After take-off, he spent his time listening to an iPod and reading his Bible.

Once the plane reached cruising altitude, the flight attendants handed out box lunches. Mr. Vereen was disappointed to find that the only substantial food in the box was a turkey sandwich, and since it was Good Friday, he couldn't eat it. It seemed at this point there was a reason that Mr. Vereen had changed seats, and that reason was baked oatmeal.

You see, early that morning as our team departed the retreat where we always stay, the owner had made baked oatmeal. She makes it the last morning of every trip, and it is delicious. But the batch that morning was behind schedule, just coming out of the oven as the vans arrived to take the group to the airport. The tired group had a four-hour drive to the airport and didn't have time to spare. They'd eaten toaster pastries while waiting for the oatmeal to bake, so they weren't hungry when the oatmeal was done. The owner insisted they take the baked oatmeal, putting it into travel containers. Jerrilee put the containers into her carry-on bag.

When Jerrilee saw that Mr. Vereen was not eating, she asked whether he liked baked oatmeal. He said he loved it! She dug the container out of her bag and served him a large portion. He ate every crumb. Just before the plane landed, he asked if he might have a little more for supper. Jerrilee provided him with another healthy serving. He thanked them several times and wished them well as they departed the plane together.

Domies

3 eggs
2 cups milk
3 cups all-purpose flour
2 tablespoons baking powder
1 teaspoon salt
1 teaspoon baking soda
Water
1/4 cup vegetable oil or lard

Beat the eggs in a medium mixing bowl. Add the milk and mix well. Set aside. Sift the flour, baking powder, salt and baking soda together in a large mixing bowl. Make a well in the center of the flour mixture. Add the egg mixture to the well and beat until smooth. Add enough water to make a moderately thick batter (slightly thinner than pancake batter). Heat the oil in a large skillet over medium heat. Add the batter. Cook over medium-high heat just until the bottom is turning golden brown. Cut into bite-size pieces with a spatula and knife as it continues to cook. You should have marble-size pieces of dough that are light brown all over. Remove from the skillet. Serve with butter and pancake syrup or sorghum.

Makes 6 servings

Note
This is my mother's recipe. She ate Domies for breakfast every morning as a child growing up in a German community. They were a cheap and filling breakfast, which was important since her widowed father had eleven children to feed! They also are known as "Doughies," "Doomies," "Smarn," "Scham," and "Swirles."

Berry-Stuffed French Toast

French Toast
10 (1-inch-thick) slices French bread
4 ounces mixed berry swirl
cream cheese, softened
2 tablespoons strawberry jam or raspberry jam
1/2 cup sliced strawberries
5 eggs
1/2 cup milk
1 tablespoon sugar
1 teaspoon vanilla bean paste

Syrup
1/2 cup strawberry jam or raspberry jam
2 to 4 tablespoons orange juice

For the French toast, cut a pocket lengthwise along one side of each slice of the bread. Combine the cream cheese and jam in a bowl and mix well. Spread 1 tablespoon of the cream cheese mixture inside each pocket.

Push a few strawberry slices into each pocket. Press the bread gently to seal the pockets.

Whisk the eggs, milk, sugar and vanilla bean paste in a bowl. Dip each piece of bread into the egg mixture. Cook on a hot griddle until golden brown on both sides, turning once. Remove to a warming dish.

For the syrup, heat the jam and orange juice in a small saucepan over low heat until heated through, whisking constantly. Serve over the French toast. Garnish with fresh blueberries, raspberries and strawberries. Dust with confectioners' sugar.

Makes 5 servings

Tall Buttery Biscuits with Gravy

Biscuits
2 cups all-purpose flour, sifted
4 teaspoons baking powder
1 teaspoon sugar
1/2 teaspoon baking soda
1/2 teaspoon salt
1/2 cup (1 stick) butter, softened
1 cup half-and-half or buttermilk
1/4 cup (1/2 stick) butter, melted

Country Sausage Gravy
1 pound bulk pork sausage
3 tablespoons flour
2 1/2 cups milk
Salt and pepper to taste

For the biscuits, preheat the oven to 425 degrees. Combine the flour, baking powder, sugar, baking soda and salt in a large bowl. Cut in 1/2 cup butter until pieces are the size of a pea or smaller. Add the half-and-half and mix just until the dough comes together. Turn the dough onto a floured surface and knead lightly to combine. Pat the dough into a 1-inch-thick circle. Cut out biscuits with a biscuit cutter. Arrange the biscuits barely touching on a nonstick baking sheet. Bake for 12 to 15 minutes or until the biscuits are golden brown. Remove from the baking sheet and brush with 1/4 cup butter.

For the gravy, brown the sausage in a skillet, stirring until crumbly; drain, reserving 3 tablespoons of the drippings in the skillet. Return the sausage to the skillet and sprinkle with the flour. Cook for 1 minute, stirring constantly. Add the milk and cook until the mixture comes to a boil, stirring constantly. Reduce the heat to medium-low and cook until the mixture is thickened and bubbly, stirring constantly. Season with salt and pepper. Serve over the biscuits.

Makes 10 to 12 biscuits with gravy

Cajun Breakfast Potatoes

1 pound fingerling potatoes or new potatoes, chopped into bite-size pieces
2 tablespoons olive oil
1 teaspoon paprika
1/2 teaspoon garlic salt
1/4 teaspoon onion powder
1/8 teaspoon cumin seeds
1/8 teaspoon oregano
1/8 teaspoon thyme
1/8 teaspoon freshly ground black pepper
2 dashes of cayenne pepper

Preheat the oven to 400 degrees. Combine the potatoes, olive oil, paprika, garlic salt, onion powder, cumin seeds, oregano, thyme, black pepper and cayenne pepper in a medium bowl and toss to coat. Spoon the mixture onto a greased baking sheet and spread evenly. Bake for 25 to 30 minutes or until the potatoes are golden brown and tender.

Makes 4 servings

Roast Chicken, Red Pepper and Havarti Pitas

4 soft Greek-style pocketless pita rounds
4 roasted red bell peppers, sliced
1 herb-roasted rotisserie chicken, sliced and boned
4 slices Havarti cheese
1/4 cup mayonnaise
1 tablespoon pesto

Preheat the oven to 350 degrees. Cut the pita bread to make eight halves. Layer one-fourth of the bell peppers, one-fourth of the chicken and one slice of the cheese on each of four halves of the pita bread. Combine the mayonnaise and pesto in a small bowl. Spread on the four remaining halves and top the sandwiches. Arrange on a baking sheet and bake for 8 to 10 minutes or until the cheese is melted.

Makes 4 sandwiches

"Rat"atouille Pizza on the Grill

Right before Thanksgiving 1998, my friends Danielle and Vern were planning to visit me in St. Maarten, arriving on Vern's birthday, as it happened.

I lived in a studio apartment with a teeny tiny kitchen. I had a small dorm-room-size refrigerator (no freezer), a two-burner cooktop, and a toaster oven. These should have limited the amount of food I could cook, but they didn't stop me. I had mastered the art of toaster-oven cooking and baking. For Vern's birthday, I decided to make cupcakes. Twenty-eight of them. I did this well ahead of time because the oven would only bake six at a time. I had twenty-eight cupcakes ready for his arrival with twenty-eight candles to go with them! Vern was quite surprised.

I showed Vern and Danielle around the island. We stopped at a little roadside pizza joint just outside of Marigot. We ordered what they called a "cream" pizza, named for the white sauce on it instead of the usual red sauce. It was so creamy and garlicky and yummy, and the crust was so crispy! We couldn't stop thinking about that scrumptious pizza.

We came up with a plan to make our own, and it required a grill. We bought shrimp and salmon, artichoke hearts, and black olives to go on a nice creamy Alfredo sauce. We made the dough and Alfredo sauce from scratch. While the dough rose, we grilled the salmon and shrimp. This worked like a charm, but some salmon and shrimp bits stuck to the grill grate. We rolled out the pizza crust and brushed it with olive oil. It puffed to a perfect golden brown on the grill. We turned it, put on the toppings, and grilled it until the bottom was also a crusty golden brown. When it was done, the hour was late, so we put the hot grill on the far side of the patio and took our pizza inside to enjoy with a nice bottle of wine.

After our feast, we were lying around, laughing and joking with full bellies, when we suddenly heard a loud clattering on the patio. Theft was not uncommon on the island, especially during low tourist season. I thought for sure someone was trying to steal my new grill but was too afraid to look behind the curtain. What if they had a gun or something! We listened intently and again heard a loud clatter. Definitely a thief, but he was sure taking his time. I was too scared to look, so I made Vern do it. That's what men are for, right?

He walked quietly to the patio door and peeked behind the curtain. He looked at us in astonishment and said, "Oh my gosh! There are five thieves out there!" I couldn't stand it anymore—I had to look. I peeked behind the curtain to see five huge rats eating scraps off the grill! I couldn't believe my eyes. They had moved the still-hot, heavy grill lid to get to the leftover bits. I flipped on the light, thinking it would scare them off, but no way were they budging. They seemed to like the pizzas on the grill just as much as we did. I was totally grossed out by the whole thing, and bleached the entire grill twice before ever using it again. But I have to admit that they have good taste . . . for scavengers!

Shrimp Scampi and Bacon Pizza on the Grill

1 tablespoon butter
1 garlic clove, minced
1 tablespoon all-purpose flour
1 cup heavy cream
1/4 teaspoon salt
16 ounces fresh or refrigerator pizza dough
All-purpose flour for dusting
1 tablespoon butter
1 garlic clove, minced
1 pound (41- to 50-count) shrimp, peeled and deveined
Salt and pepper to taste
10 ounces frozen chopped spinach, thawed and drained
8 slices bacon, crisp-cooked and crumbled
8 ounces mozzarella cheese, shredded
2 ounces Parmesan cheese, grated
2 tablespoons fresh parsley, chopped
Crushed red pepper flakes to taste (optional)

Grease the grill rack and preheat the grill to medium. Melt 1 tablespoon butter in a small saucepan. Add 1 garlic clove and sauté until tender. Stir in 1 tablespoon flour and cook for 1 minute, stirring constantly. Add the cream and 1/4 teaspoon salt and mix well. Cook until thickened and bubbly. Remove from the heat and set aside. Shape the dough into four 6- to 8-inch round pizza crusts. Dust with flour and place on baking sheets.

Melt 1 tablespoon butter in a skillet over medium-high heat. Add 1 garlic clove and the shrimp and sauté for 3 minutes or until the shrimp turn pink and the garlic is tender. Season with salt and pepper.

Grill the crusts for 5 to 8 minutes or until the bottoms of the crusts are golden brown. Turn and spread one-fourth of the white sauce over each crust. Press the excess moisture from the spinach. Top each crust with equal amounts of the shrimp, spinach, bacon, mozzarella cheese and Parmesan cheese. Grill for 5 to 10 minutes or until the bottoms of the crusts are golden brown and the cheeses are melted. Serve immediately or keep warm in a 200-degree oven. Top with parsley and red pepper flakes just before serving.

Makes 4 servings

Croque Monsieur

8 slices Italian boule or French loaf bread
4 thick slices ham
1 tablespoon butter
1 tablespoon all-purpose flour
1/2 cup half-and-half
1/4 cup white wine or sherry
2 teaspoons Dijon mustard
1/4 teaspoon salt, or to taste
Dash of white pepper
8 to 12 ounces Gruyère cheese, grated

Preheat the broiler to 450 degrees. Make four sandwiches from the bread and ham. Arrange the sandwiches on a baking sheet. Melt the butter in a small saucepan and stir in the flour. Cook for 1 minute, stirring constantly. Stir in the half-and-half, wine, Dijon mustard, salt and white pepper. Spoon equal amounts of the sauce over each sandwich, spreading it to the edges. Top each sandwich with 2 to 3 ounces of the cheese. Broil for 7 to 8 minutes or until the cheese is light golden brown. Do not leave the sandwiches unattended, as they burn quickly. Let stand to cool slightly. Serve warm.

Makes 4 servings

Duck Breast Sandwiches

Raspberry Dijon Vinaigrette
1 tablespoon raspberry white balsamic vinegar
1 teaspoon Dijon mustard
1 teaspoon honey
1 teaspoon minced shallot
1 to 2 tablespoons olive oil
Salt and freshly cracked pepper to taste

Sandwiches
2 tablespoons butter
1 large onion, chopped
Salt and pepper to taste
2 fully cooked smoked duck breasts
1 baguette
2 tablespoons fig jam
1 tablespoon Dijon mustard
4 ounces Gruyère cheese, sliced
2 cups mixed baby salad greens

For the vinaigrette, whisk the vinegar, 1 teaspoon Dijon mustard, the honey and shallot in a small bowl. Add the olive oil in a fine stream, whisking constantly until emulsified. Season with salt and pepper. Set aside.

For the sandwiches, melt the butter in a skillet over medium-high heat. Add the onion and cook until caramelized, stirring occasionally. Season with salt and pepper. Let stand until cool. Preheat the oven to 350 degrees. Cut the duck into 1/4-inch strips. Cut the baguette lengthwise into halves. Spread the fig jam on the top half of the bread. Spread 1 tablespoon Dijon mustard on the bottom half. Arrange the baguette halves on a large baking sheet. Layer the duck, onion and cheese over the Dijon mustard. Bake just until the bread is crusty and the cheese is melted.

Toss the vinaigrette with the salad greens. Arrange the greens on the bottom half of the baguette and cover with the top half. Cut into four equal portions. Serve warm.

Makes 4 servings

King of Club Sandwiches

6 slices whole wheat bread, toasted
3 tablespoons mayonnaise
2 thick slices Bavarian ham
4 slices Swiss cheese
1 tomato, thinly sliced
2 hard-cooked eggs, sliced
8 slices crisp-cooked bacon
1/2 cup spring lettuce mix

For each sandwich, spread each of three toast slices with 1/2 tablespoon of the mayonnaise. Place one slice of toast on a work surface. Layer with one slice of the ham, one slice of the cheese, half the tomato slices, one slice of toast, half the egg slices, one slice of the cheese, half the bacon and half the lettuce. Top with the remaining toast, mayonnaise side down. Skewer opposite corners of each sandwich with wooden picks. Cut the sandwiches diagonally into halves.

Makes 2 servings

Italian Steak Panini

2 (8-ounce) New York strip steaks or rib-eye steaks
1 tablespoon Italian seasoning
Salt and pepper to taste
2 large portobello mushrooms
2 tablespoons butter
1 large sweet onion, sliced
1/4 cup mayonnaise
1 tablespoon finely chopped sun-dried tomatoes
1 tablespoon pesto
1 tablespoon finely grated Parmesan cheese
4 Italian panini rolls, split
8 large spinach leaves
8 slices provolone cheese or fontina cheese

Preheat the grill to medium-high. Season the steaks with the Italian seasoning, salt and pepper. Grill the steaks until between medium-rare and medium (145 degrees to 160 degrees). Grill mushrooms with the steaks. Let both stand to cool for 20 minutes. Melt the butter in a large skillet. Add the onion and sauté until caramelized. Set aside. Combine the mayonnaise, tomatoes, pesto and Parmesan cheese in a small bowl. Cut the steaks and mushrooms into 1/4- to 1/2-inch-long slices. Pat the mushrooms dry. Layer equal amounts of the meat, mushrooms and onion on the bottom half of each panini roll. Top each roll with two spinach leaves and two slices of provolone cheese. Spread one-fourth of the mayonnaise mixture over the top half of each panini roll and use these to top the sandwiches. Coat a panini press with olive oil. Toast the sandwiches according to the manufacturer's directions until the cheese is melted. Serve warm.

Makes 4 servings

Oyster Po' Boys

1/4 cup dark beer
1/4 cup heavy cream
1 pound shucked oysters
3/4 cup all-purpose flour
1/4 cup cornmeal
1/2 teaspoon garlic salt
1/2 teaspoon pepper
Vegetable oil for frying
1 tablespoon butter
2 large hoagie buns, split
1 cup creamy coleslaw
Tartar sauce

Combine the beer and cream in a large glass bowl. Add the oysters and marinate for 30 minutes. Combine the flour, cornmeal, garlic salt and pepper in a sealable plastic bag. Remove the oysters from the marinade. Add the oysters to the bag and seal; toss to coat well. Heat the oil in a skillet over medium heat. Shake any excess flour from the oysters. Fry the oysters in the oil for 5 to 8 minutes or until golden brown; drain on paper towels. Melt the butter in a large skillet. Add the bun halves and toast to golden brown. Arrange the bun bottoms on a serving plate. Spread 1/2 cup coleslaw on each. Top with the oysters. Drizzle with tartar sauce and cover with the tops of the buns.

Makes 2 servings

Beef Wellington

Mom's Meat Loaf

Thai Lettuce Wraps

Armenian Shish Kabobs

Smoked Peking Duck

Barbecue Boston Butt

Pork Chops Stuffed with Smoked Gouda and Apple

Sesame Seared Ahi Tuna Steaks

Cedar Plank Salmon Steaks in Asian Marinade

Spanish Paella

Seafood au Gratin

Hearty Black Bean Burritos

Cheesy Chicken Portobello Lasagna

Pasta Sfoglia Pollo con Spinaci

Dinner Entrées

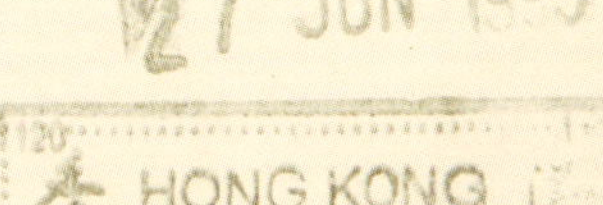

Beef Wellington

Beef

$2^1/_2$ pounds beef tenderloin, at room temperature
4 tablespoons butter
2 shallots, minced
$1^1/_2$ pounds fresh mushrooms, finely chopped
$^1/_4$ cup sherry
Salt and pepper to taste
1 (17-ounce) package frozen puff pastry, thawed
1 egg yolk, beaten

Green Peppercorn Sauce

2 tablespoons butter
2 tablespoons all-purpose flour
$1^1/_2$ cups heavy cream
$^1/_2$ cup sherry or white wine
1 tablespoon green peppercorns in brine, drained
Salt and pepper to taste

For the beef, preheat the oven to 425 degrees. Melt 2 tablespoons of the butter in a skillet over medium-high heat. Add the beef and cook until seared, turning to brown all sides. Let stand at room temperature.

Reduce the heat to medium and melt the remaining 2 tablespoons butter in the skillet. Add the shallots, mushrooms and sherry and sauté until the vegetables are tender. Drain two-thirds of the mixture well, reserving one-third of the mixture in the skillet for the sauce.

Roll out the puff pastry, sealing the seam to make one sheet. Spread the drained mushroom mixture in the center of the pastry to within 2 to 3 inches from the edge. Position the beef in the center. Fold the puff pastry around the beef and press to seal the seams. Make sure the seams are not too thick; trim any excess dough. Roll the excess dough and cut into petal shapes. Arrange into a flower design on top of the pastry. Place in a 9×13-inch baking dish. Brush the pastry with the egg yolk. Bake for 25 to 30 minutes or until the pastry is a rich golden brown. Let stand for 15 minutes before slicing.

For the sauce, heat the reserved mushroom mixture in the skillet. Add the butter and heat until melted. Sprinkle with the flour and mix well. Stir in the cream and sherry and cook until thickened, stirring constantly. Add the peppercorns, salt and pepper. Cut the beef into slices and serve with the sauce.

Makes 6 servings

Note

This recipe is classically made with foie gras mixed with the mushrooms. Some people protest foie gras for ethical reasons. This decision is up to you, of course, but I left it out, since it's just as delicious without it.

Well-Traveled Beef Wellington

The first time I made Beef Wellington was with my friend Danielle. She is my cooking buddy and lifelong best friend. One night we wanted something fancy, so we decided on individual Beef Wellingtons. We started with a basic recipe, but we added a pinch of this, a dash of that, plus a green peppercorn sauce, and voila! A masterpiece! I expanded the recipe to use a whole tenderloin because anyone who found out I was making it wanted to come for dinner.

I made the mistake of making it for my friend Paul. I met him through my friend Clay while living in England. He is originally from South Africa but eventually moved to Chicago to work for a big advertising firm. Chicago is where I first made my Beef Wellington for him. From then on, whenever I came for a visit, no matter how short the stay, he demanded my Beef Wellington.

He repaid the favors by taking me back to his hometown of George, South Africa, to visit his parents. Clay went with us as well. It was an amazing trip. So many things were so different from where I grew up. For instance, when we walked out onto their back deck and looked at the bush down below, there were monkeys everywhere, sitting in the trees looking at us. And as a matter of fact, the house had bars on all the windows and doors to keep the monkeys out. They would try to sneak in and raid your pantry and refrigerator! I was also intrigued, if not terrified, by the huge whip hanging by their back door. This was to be used to break the back of a snake, should one get inside the house. Nor was I comforted when I stepped out the front door one night to see a scorpion scurry across the sidewalk. It was all worth the risk, though, when we went for a drive and I saw wild zebras, springboks, and wildebeests on the way to collect spectacular shells along the shores of the Indian Ocean.

Paul's parents were some of the loveliest people I have ever met and were exceptional hosts. They put on a *brai*, Afrikaans for "barbecue," for Clay and me, grilling steak, lamb, and springbok sausage. As a thank-you, I made my Beef Wellington. We gathered at the table and carved the beef. At the first bite, there were pleasurable moans, as they savored the tender meat, duxelle, and flaky pastry, with bursts of flavor from green peppercorns. His mother, Marion swallowed, then said in Afrikaans, "Dit prue net soos 'n Engel op my tong gepiepie het." That translates to, "It tastes as though an angel has just poo pood on my tongue." What a cute, whimsical saying, assuming that angel poo is tasty. Anyway, I took it as a compliment.

A few months later, Paul's birthday was near, but work duties prevented me from seeing him. I came up with the idea of preparing and freezing individual Beef Wellingtons and sending them via overnight delivery. It worked like a charm, and he got his Beef Wellington after all.

Mom's Meat Loaf

Meat Loaf
1 tablespoon butter
1/2 cup chopped onion
1/4 cup chopped red bell pepper or green bell pepper
2 pounds ground chuck
2 eggs
1/3 cup ketchup
1/3 cup rolled oats
1 tablespoon brown sugar
1 teaspoon salt
1 teaspoon pepper

Sauce
1/2 cup ketchup
1 tablespoon brown sugar
1/2 teaspoon brown mustard
1/4 teaspoon freshly ground pepper

For the meat loaf, preheat the oven to 350 degrees. Melt the butter in a small skillet. Add the onion and bell pepper and sauté until tender. Combine with the ground chuck, eggs, ketchup, oats, brown sugar, salt and pepper in a large bowl and mix just until combined; do not overmix or the meat loaf will be tough. Press into a loaf pan. Bake for 1 hour.

For the sauce, combine the ketchup, brown sugar, mustard and pepper in a small bowl. Spoon the sauce over the meat loaf. Increase the oven temperature to 375 degrees. Bake for 20 minutes longer. Let stand for 15 minutes before slicing.

Makes 6 servings

Note
No matter where I traveled in the world, whenever I came home I always begged Mom to make her good old-fashioned meat loaf. Nothing beats classic American comfort food!

Thai Lettuce Wraps

1 pound flank steak, or 3 large chicken breasts
1/4 cup soy sauce
2 tablespoons hoisin sauce
2 tablespoons dark brown sugar
2 tablespoons rice wine vinegar
1 tablespoon sherry
1 teaspoon sesame oil
1 teaspoon chili oil
2 garlic cloves, crushed
2 tablespoons peanut oil
2 cups cooked sushi rice
8 leaves butter lettuce
1 large carrot, shredded
1 cup bean sprouts
2 scallions, chopped
1/4 cup cilantro, chopped

Tenderize the flank steak and cut into 1-inch strips. Combine the soy sauce, hoisin sauce, brown sugar, vinegar, sherry, sesame oil, chili oil and garlic in a large bowl. Add the steak and turn to coat. Marinate in the refrigerator for 30 minutes to 2 hours. Remove the steak and discard the marinade. Heat the peanut oil in a large skillet or wok over high heat. Add the steak and stir-fry for 3 to 4 minutes or until brown. Remove to a serving plate.

Lay a lettuce leaf flat and place 1/4 cup of the rice in the center. Top with one-eighth each of the steak, carrot, bean sprouts, scallions and cilantro. Fold in the ends and roll to enclose the filling. Repeat with the remaining lettuce leaves and filling. Serve with sweet Thai chili sauce and hoisin sauce.

Makes 4 servings

Armenian Shish Kabobs

Yogurt Sauce
1/2 cup plain yogurt
1 garlic clove, mashed to a paste
1 tablespoon chopped parsley

Kabobs
1 1/2 pounds ground lamb
1 small onion, finely chopped
2 garlic cloves, crushed
2 tablespoons fresh mint, chopped
1 teaspoon fresh oregano, chopped
1/2 teaspoon turmeric
1/2 teaspoon salt
1/2 teaspoon pepper
1 egg
1/4 cup dry bread crumbs
8 soft pita rounds or lavash
Mixed baby greens
Fresh parsley

For the sauce, combine the yogurt, garlic and parsley in a small bowl. Set aside.

For the kabobs, preheat the grill to 350 degrees. Soak eight wooden skewers in water to cover. Combine the lamb, onion, garlic, mint, oregano, turmeric, salt, pepper, egg and bread crumbs in a large bowl and mix gently but thoroughly. Do not overmix or the kabobs will be tough. Divide the lamb mixture evenly into eight mounds. Shape each mound around a skewer. Grill the kabobs for 20 to 30 minutes or until the lamb is cooked through. Serve the kabobs with the pita bread, baby greens, parsley and yogurt sauce.

Makes 8 servings

Smoked Peking Duck

1 (5- to 6-pound) duck
1 orange, cut into chunks
1 sweet onion, cut into chunks
Salt and pepper to taste
1/4 cup soy sauce
1/4 cup honey
2 tablespoons molasses
Juice of 1/2 orange
2 tablespoons sherry
1 teaspoon grated orange zest
8 whole cloves
4 peppercorns
Hoisin sauce
Mandarin pancakes
2 scallions, julienned

Preheat a smoker to 275 degrees. Remove the giblets from the duck. Discard the giblets or reserve for another use. Pat the duck dry with paper towels. Stuff with the orange and onion. Season with salt and pepper. Place the duck in the smoker away from direct heat. Combine the soy sauce, honey, molasses, orange juice, sherry, orange zest, cloves and peppercorns in a bowl and mix well. Baste the duck with this mixture every 15 minutes. Smoke for 3 to 4 hours or to 170 degrees on a meat thermometer. Let stand until cool enough to handle. Cut the meat from the bones. To serve, spread 1 tablespoon hoisin sauce over each mandarin pancake and top with the duck and scallions. Roll to enclose the filling and serve immediately.

Makes 4 servings

Barbecue Boston Butt

"Doctored-Up" Barbecue Sauce
2 tablespoons butter
1/2 Vidalia onion, chopped
3 garlic cloves, minced
1/2 cup packed dark brown sugar
2 tablespoons soy sauce
1/2 cup ketchup
2 cups bottled barbecue sauce
1/2 cup water

Pork
1 (6- to 8-pound) Boston butt roast, trimmed and wrapped in kitchen twine
4 to 6 tablespoons of your favorite grill seasoning

For the sauce, melt the butter in a medium saucepan over medium heat. Add the onion and sauté for 2 to 3 minutes or until tender. Add the garlic and sauté for 1 to 2 minutes longer. Add the brown sugar, soy sauce, ketchup, barbecue sauce and water and bring to a boil. Reduce the heat to low and simmer for 20 to 30 minutes.

For the pork, soak sassafras, hickory or apple wood in water for 2 hours. Prepare a medium-hot fire from the soaked wood in a rotisserie-style grill that can maintain a temperature of 250 to 300 degrees. Let the pork come to room temperature. Coat all over with the grill seasoning, pressing it into the creases of the roast. Skewer the roast on a rotisserie spit. Grill for 4 to 5 hours or to 165 degrees on an instant-read thermometer. Let the roast stand for 10 to 20 minutes before slicing. Serve with the warm sauce.

Makes 12 servings

A "Proper" Barbecue Grill

After nine months of living in England, I began to get really homesick. Luckily, my parents decided to come for a monthlong visit. My friends had already experienced my father's barbecue in St. Maarten, and they knew a visit from my parents meant that good grub was coming! Just one problem—grilling is not so common in England, and our "grill" held just three or four hamburgers and wasn't nearly big enough for a pork butt.

My father scoured Gillingham, Kent, for a "proper" grill, finally giving up in favor of building his own. He used a stainless steel washing machine tub found at a used parts shop for the base—it was ideal for holding the wood and withstanding heat, and the holes would ventilate the fire. Next, he found a stainless steel refrigerator rack to sit on the tub. He used chicken wire to build a ring, which he covered with foil to support a lid. The lid came from a metal trash can. It looked hilarious, and my friends referred to it as "the redneck barbecue."

Now we needed the right flavoring for the meat. My dad likes hickory but none could be found. Then I remembered an apple orchard nearby. We set off with trash bags to beg for apple tree limbs. The orchard owner was puzzled, saying, "You want to cut limbs off our apple trees?" We explained that we wanted dead branches from the ground to flavor the meat we were grilling. "I heard you Americans do that," added a passerby, overhearing the transaction. The owner eventually let us gather two bags of branches.

Next, the meat. None of the British cuts was quite equivalent to a Boston butt, but we took a guess and came home with two something-or-other pork roasts.

Dad fired up the new grill and tended it for hours while Mom and I made barbecue sauce, side dishes, and more. Everyone in the neighborhood could smell the wonderful aroma of the meat and the apple wood smoke. Dad is a master at grilling, even in England.

Finally, my friends gathered around the table and Dad took the meat off the grill. Those poor roasts didn't have a chance! They were gone in five minutes. And the "redneck grill" had proven itself, becoming a legend among the students who followed us in England. And so it stayed there, and it's probably still making people happy in eastern England.

Pork Chops Stuffed with Smoked Gouda and Apple

Pork Chops
4 slices maple-flavored bacon, cut into 1/2-inch pieces
1 apple, peeled and finely chopped
2 tablespoons finely chopped shallot
2 tablespoons finely chopped celery
1 teaspoon fresh sage, finely chopped
1/4 cup dry bread crumbs
2 tablespoons chicken stock
1 egg, beaten
1/2 cup (2 ounces) shredded smoked Gouda cheese
Salt and freshly ground pepper to taste
4 (1-inch-thick) pork chops
All-purpose flour for dusting
1 tablespoon butter

Onion Pan Sauce
1 sweet onion, thinly sliced
1/3 cup balsamic vinegar
1/4 cup honey
2 tablespoons Dijon mustard
2 tablespoons sherry
Salt and pepper to taste

For the pork chops, preheat the oven to 350 degrees. Cook the bacon in a large ovenproof skillet over medium heat until brown and crispy; remove the bacon and set aside on paper towels. Drain, reserving 1 tablespoon of the drippings in the skillet. Add the apple, shallot and celery and sauté for 5 minutes or until tender. Add the sage and sauté for 1 minute longer. Remove from the heat and let cool slightly. Add the bread crumbs, stock, egg, cheese, salt and pepper and mix well. Cut a pocket horizontally in each pork chop. Spoon one-fourth of the stuffing into each pork chop. Season with salt and pepper and coat with flour. Melt the butter in the skillet. Add the pork chops and sauté for 3 to 5 minutes per side or until brown. Place the skillet in the oven. Bake for 20 to 22 minutes or to 160 degrees on a meat thermometer. Remove the pork chops to a serving plate and keep warm.

For the sauce, sauté the onion in the skillet over medium heat until caramelized. Add the vinegar and cook until reduced by one-half. Stir in the honey, Dijon mustard and sherry and heat through. Season with salt and pepper. Drizzle over the pork.

Makes 4 servings

Sesame Seared Ahi Tuna Steaks

2 tablespoons soy sauce
2 tablespoons sherry
1 tablespoon sugar
2 teaspoons sesame oil
2 garlic cloves, crushed
1/2 teaspoon wasabi powder or wasabi paste
4 (8-ounce) Ahi tuna steaks, cut 1 inch thick
1/4 cup white sesame seeds
1/4 cup black sesame seeds
2 tablespoons peanut oil

Combine the soy sauce, sherry, sugar, sesame oil, garlic and wasabi powder in a large bowl and mix well. Add the tuna and turn to coat. Marinate for 15 to 30 minutes. Combine the sesame seeds in a shallow dish. Coat the tuna with the sesame seeds. Heat the peanut oil in a large skillet over medium-high heat. Sear the tuna for 1 to 1 1/2 minutes per side or until rare to medium-rare. Remove from the heat and serve immediately.

Makes 4 servings

Cedar Plank Salmon Steaks in Asian Marinade

1 tablespoon light peanut oil
1 shallot, minced
3 garlic cloves, crushed
2 teaspoons minced fresh ginger
1/2 cup hoisin sauce
1/2 cup orange marmalade
2 tablespoons soy sauce
2 tablespoons sherry or mirin
2 tablespoons dark brown sugar
4 salmon steaks

Soak a large cedar plank in water to cover for 2 hours prior to use. Heat the peanut oil in a small saucepan over medium heat. Add the shallot, garlic and ginger and sauté until tender. Stir in the hoisin sauce, marmalade, soy sauce, sherry and brown sugar and heat through. Remove from the heat and let stand to cool. Combine the salmon and the sauce in a glass dish or sealable plastic bag. Marinate the salmon for 1 1/2 to 2 hours. Preheat one side of the grill to medium-high. Place the planks on the other side of the grill for indirect grilling. Arrange the salmon on the plank. Grill over indirect heat for 20 to 30 minutes or until the fish flakes easily with a fork. Serve immediately.

Makes 4 servings

Spanish Paella

1 tablespoon vegetable oil
4 ounces chorizo
1/2 Vidalia onion, chopped
1/4 cup chopped red bell pepper
3 garlic cloves, minced
2 small tomatoes, peeled and chopped
Salt and pepper to taste
1 cup arborio rice
2 1/2 cups chicken broth
1/2 cup cooking sherry
1 teaspoon saffron threads
1 teaspoon sweet paprika
8 littleneck clams in shells
14 mussels in shells
12 large shrimp, peeled and deveined, with tails left on
4 ounces calamari, cleaned and cut into rings
1/2 cup frozen peas

Heat the oil in a large heavy skillet over medium heat. Add the chorizo and sauté for 10 minutes or until cooked through. Remove the chorizo to a bowl using a slotted spoon. Sauté the onion and bell pepper in the skillet until tender. Add the garlic and sauté until golden brown. Stir in the tomatoes and cook until the flavors have blended. Season with salt and pepper. Add the rice and stir to coat. Add the broth, sherry, saffron and paprika and simmer for 10 minutes, stirring occasionally. Add the clams, mussels, shrimp, calamari and chorizo, pushing them down into the mixture. Simmer without stirring for 15 to 20 minutes or until the rice is al dente and the clams and mussel shells open. Scatter the peas over the top and simmer for 5 minutes longer. Remove from the heat and let stand for 5 to 10 minutes. Serve with crusty bread and sangria.

Makes 6 servings

Seafood au Gratin

8 ounces lump crab meat, drained and flaked
8 ounces medium shrimp, peeled and deveined
8 ounces small scallops
2 tablespoons butter
1 shallot, minced
1 garlic clove, minced
2 tablespoons all-purpose flour
1 cup heavy cream
1/2 cup white wine
2 tablespoons sherry or Cognac
1 tablespoon Worcestershire sauce
1/4 cup Dijon mustard
2 tablespoons chopped roasted red bell pepper
1/2 cup (2 ounces) grated Parmesan cheese
4 ounces Gruyère cheese, grated
1/4 cup dry bread crumbs

Preheat the oven to 400 degrees. Combine the crab, shrimp and scallops in a medium bowl. Melt the butter in a medium saucepan. Add the shallot and garlic and sauté until tender. Stir in the flour until smooth. Add the cream, wine, sherry, Worcestershire sauce and Dijon mustard and mix well. Cook over medium heat until thick and bubbly, whisking constantly. Add the seafood and cook for 2 minutes, stirring frequently. Remove from the heat. Stir in the bell pepper and Parmesan cheese. Spoon into au gratin dishes. Top with the Gruyère cheese and bread crumbs. Bake for 15 minutes or until the cheese is golden brown and the sauce is bubbly.

Makes 4 servings

Hearty Black Bean Burritos

2 tablespoons olive oil
1 small onion, chopped
1 jalapeño chile, finely chopped
3 garlic cloves, minced
2 teaspoons ground cumin
1 teaspoon ground coriander
1/4 teaspoon cayenne pepper
1 (14-ounce) can diced tomatoes
2 (15-ounce) cans black beans, drained and rinsed
2 cups chicken broth
1/2 cup medium grain brown rice
Salt and pepper to taste
8 flour tortillas
8 ounces Colby Jack cheese, shredded

Heat the olive oil in a large skillet. Add the onion and jalapeño chile and sauté until tender. Add the garlic and sauté for 2 minutes. Add the cumin, coriander and cayenne pepper and sauté for 1 minute. Stir in the tomatoes, black beans, broth and rice. Simmer for 20 minutes or until the liquid is absorbed and the rice is tender. Preheat the oven to 350 degrees. Season the rice mixture with salt and pepper. Divide the mixture equally among the tortillas. Roll to enclose the filling. Arrange in a baking dish. Top with the cheese. Bake for 10 to 15 minutes or until the cheese is melted.

Makes 4 servings

Note

I was on a very strict budget my first two semesters of medical school, so beans and rice became a main staple in my diet because they are cheap, cheap, cheap! I didn't mind, though. These burritos are so tasty that I still make them even though the budget is not as tight. They are healthful eating, too!

Cheesy Chicken Portobello Lasagna

Garlicky Cream Sauce

1/2 cup (1 stick) butter
1 onion, chopped
3 garlic cloves, minced
1/2 cup all-purpose flour
5 1/2 cups milk
1 cup heavy cream
1 1/2 cups chicken broth
1 cup (4 ounces) grated Parmesan cheese

Lasagna

4 portobello mushrooms, sliced 1/2 inch thick
2 eggs
16 ounces ricotta cheese
16 uncooked lasagna noodles
1 roasted chicken, deboned and chopped
16 ounces mozzarella cheese, shredded
4 ounces Parmesan cheese, grated
6 ounces frozen spinach, thawed and drained
1/2 cup water

For the sauce, melt the butter in a skillet. Add the onion and garlic and sauté until tender. Stir in the flour. Cook until smooth, whisking constantly. Add the milk, cream and broth. Cook until thickened, stirring constantly. Stir in the cheese.

For the lasagna, roast the mushroom slices on a baking sheet in a 400-degree oven for 10 minutes. Reduce the heat to 375 degrees. Beat the eggs and ricotta cheese in a bowl. Spread 1/2 cup of the garlic sauce in a greased extra-large extra-deep baking pan. Arrange four of the noodles in a single layer over the sauce in the pan. Layer with one-third of the ricotta cheese mixture, one-half of the chicken, one-fourth of the remaining sauce, one-fourth of the mozzarella cheese, one-fourth of the Parmesan cheese, four noodles, one-third of the ricotta cheese, all the mushrooms, all the spinach, one-fourth of the remaining sauce, one-fourth of the mozzarella cheese, one-fourth of the Parmesan cheese, four noodles, the remaining ricotta cheese, the remaining chicken, one-fourth of the mozzarella cheese, one-fourth of the Parmesan cheese, four noodles and the remaining sauce, mozzarella cheese and Parmesan cheese. Pour the water around the edges of the lasagna. Cover with foil. Bake for 45 to 50 minutes. Uncover and bake for 10 minutes longer. Let stand for 30 minutes before serving.

Makes 8 servings

Pasta Sfoglia Pollo con Spinaci

8 ounces mascarpone cheese, softened
1/4 cup sun-dried tomatoes, chopped
1/3 cup thawed well-drained frozen chopped spinach
1 (6-ounce) jar marinated artichoke hearts, drained and chopped
4 ounce asiago cheese, shredded
2 garlic cloves, crushed
1 tablespoon pesto
6 boneless skinless chicken breasts
Salt and freshly ground pepper to taste
2 sheets frozen puff pastry, thawed
1 egg, beaten

Preheat the oven to 375 degrees. Combine the mascarpone cheese, tomatoes, spinach, artichoke hearts, asiago cheese, garlic and pesto in a medium bowl and mix well. Season the chicken with salt and pepper.

Unfold the pastry on a floured surface. Cut each sheet into halves. Cut three of the halves into halves again so you have six equal pieces and one oblong piece. Roll the six equal pieces into 8-inch squares. Divide the cheese mixture among the pastry squares. Top each with a chicken breast. Brush the edge of the pastry with the beaten egg. Fold the edges of the pastry over the chicken breast, sealing the seams well. Arrange the bundles seam side down 2 inches apart on a nonstick baking sheet. Cut decorative shapes from the remaining pastry and top the bundles. Brush each bundle with the beaten egg. Bake for 30 minutes or until the pastry is golden brown and the chicken is cooked through. Let stand for 5 to 10 minutes before serving.

Makes 6 servings

Roasted Vegetable Medley

Roasted Asparagus with Balsamic Glaze

Orange- and Brandy-Glazed Carrots

Cauliflower au Gratin

Haricots Verts with Pancetta, Pesto and Pine Nuts

Creamed Peas with Cremini Mushrooms

Potato Wedges with Sweet Thai Chili Sauce

Gruyère au Gratin Potatoes

Garlic and Gouda Mashed Potatoes

Sweet Potato Casserole

Stewed Tomatoes

Oyster Dressing

Three Cheese and Wild Mushroom Risotto

Gnocchi with Gorgonzola and Walnuts

Side Items

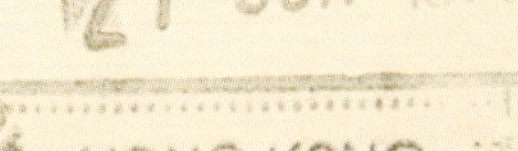

Roasted Vegetable Medley

1 Japanese eggplant
Salt to taste
1 zucchini
1 yellow squash
8 asparagus spears
1 yellow bell pepper
1 red bell pepper
8 ounces cremini mushrooms
1 sweet onion
1 teaspoon garlic powder
1/4 cup extra-virgin olive oil
Freshly ground pepper to taste
2 ounces Parmesan cheese, grated

Preheat the broiler to 500 degrees. Cut the eggplant into halves lengthwise and sprinkle the cut sides with salt. Place in a colander and let drain for 20 to 30 minutes. Rinse, dry and cut into bite-size pieces. Cut the zucchini, squash, asparagus, bell peppers, mushrooms and onion into bite-size pieces.

Combine the vegetables with the garlic powder, olive oil, salt and pepper in a large bowl and toss to coat. Spread the vegetables in a single layer on a nonstick baking sheet. Broil for 6 minutes. Turn the vegetables and broil for 6 to 10 minutes longer or until the vegetables are crisp and beginning to brown. Spoon into a serving dish. Sprinkle with the cheese immediately and serve hot.

Makes 4 servings

Roasted Asparagus with Balsamic Glaze

1 pound asparagus
2 tablespoons extra-virgin olive oil
2 tablespoons balsamic vinegar
2 tablespoons honey
1 garlic clove, minced
Coarse sea salt to taste

Preheat the oven to 425 degrees. Snap off the woody ends of each asparagus spear. Arrange the asparagus in a single layer on a nonstick baking sheet. Drizzle with the olive oil. Roast for 10 minutes.

Combine the vinegar, honey and garlic in a small saucepan over medium heat. Heat until the honey is combined and the mixture is warm, stirring constantly. Drizzle the mixture over the asparagus. Season with the salt. Return the asparagus to the oven and roast for 2 to 3 minutes longer. Serve immediately.

Makes 4 servings

Orange- and Brandy-Glazed Carrots

1 cup water
1 pound baby carrots
2 tablespoons butter
1 teaspoon grated fresh ginger
1 tablespoon dark brown sugar
1 tablespoon honey
1/4 cup fresh orange juice
1 teaspoon grated orange zest
2 tablespoons brandy
Salt to taste
1 tablespoon chopped fresh parsley or cilantro

Bring the water to a boil in a medium saucepan over high heat. Add the carrots and boil until tender-crisp. Drain and set aside. Melt the butter in a small saucepan over medium heat. Add the ginger and sauté until tender. Add the brown sugar, honey, orange juice, orange zest, brandy and salt and mix well. Bring to a boil and cook until the brown sugar is melted and the mixture is slightly reduced and thickened. Reduce the heat to low and add the carrots to the sauce. Cook until heated through, basting the carrots frequently. Mix in the parsley and remove from the heat. Spoon into a serving dish and serve immediately.

Makes 4 servings

Cauliflower au Gratin

1 head cauliflower
Salt to taste
1/4 cup mayonnaise
2 tablespoons prepared horseradish
1 garlic clove, crushed
1 tablespoon fresh tarragon, finely chopped
Pepper to taste
1 cup (4 ounces) shredded Gruyère cheese

Preheat the oven to 350 degrees. Cut the cauliflower into bite-size pieces. Bring a stockpot of salted water to a boil. Add the cauliflower and boil until tender-crisp; drain. Rinse the cauliflower with cold water to stop the cooking process. Set aside. Combine the mayonnaise, horseradish, garlic and tarragon in a small bowl and mix well. Arrange the cauliflower in a greased baking dish and spread the mayonnaise mixture over the top. Season with salt and pepper. Sprinkle with the cheese. Bake for 18 to 20 minutes or until the cheese is melted and light brown.

Makes 6 servings

Haricots Verts with Pancetta, Pesto and Pine Nuts

Salt to taste
1 pound haricots verts
1 tablespoon olive oil
4 ounces pancetta, diced
2 tablespoons pesto
Pepper to taste
2 tablespoons pine nuts, toasted

Bring lightly salted water to a boil in a stockpot. Add the beans and boil for 3 to 4 minutes or until the beans are tender-crisp; drain. Rinse the beans with cold water to stop the cooking process. Set aside. Heat the olive oil in a large skillet over medium-high heat. Add the pancetta and cook for 3 to 4 minutes or until crisp. Add the beans and pesto and cook for 1 to 2 minutes. Season with salt and pepper. Remove from the heat and toss with the pine nuts. Serve immediately.

Makes 4 servings

Creamed Peas with Cremini Mushrooms

2 tablespoons butter
2 garlic cloves, minced
1 pound cremini mushrooms, cut into quarters
1 (10-ounce) package frozen peas
2 tablespoons heavy cream
1 tablespoon marsala
Salt and pepper to taste

Melt the butter in a large skillet over medium-high heat. Add the garlic and mushrooms and sauté just until tender. Add the frozen peas, cream and wine and bring to a boil. Cook until the liquid is reduced by one-half. Season with salt and pepper. Serve immediately.

Makes 4 servings

Potato Wedges with Sweet Thai Chili Sauce

4 large baking potatoes
1/4 cup extra-virgin olive oil
1 teaspoon seasoned salt
1/4 teaspoon pepper
1/4 teaspoon paprika
Sweet Thai chili sauce
Sour cream

Preheat the oven to 425 degrees. Scrub the potatoes and pat dry. Cut the potatoes into 1-inch-thick slices lengthwise. Toss the potatoes with the olive oil, salt, pepper and paprika in a large bowl. Arrange the potatoes in a single layer on a nonstick baking sheet. Bake for 30 to 40 minutes. Turn the potatoes and bake for 15 to 20 minutes longer or until tender and golden brown. Serve hot with sweet Thai chili sauce and sour cream for dipping.

Makes 6 servings

Potato Wedges: The Perfect After-Snorkeling Snack

When I told my friend Laura, a family practice resident in Louisiana, about my upcoming general practice rotation in Sydney, Australia, she decided it was time for an adventure. She joined me for a couple of weeks, arriving in Sydney from Louisiana the day I arrived from Tasmania.

We were oriented at the practitioners' office and learned that the following Monday was a holiday and that the office would be closed. We were in Australia with a three-day weekend! What to do?

After some on-line searching, we found an affordable flight to Cairns, where we would snorkel the Great Barrier Reef! On the big weekend, we arrived in Cairns and booked a flight to Moore Reef with plans to return by boat. Pricey, but when would we have the chance again? Let's go! Let's do it!

The next morning we got up early and headed for the heliport. Among the safety measures was weighing the passengers—that was us! The horror! I don't care if you are a size 2 or 20, the only time people (other than your physician) should know a woman's weight is if she's getting ready to be an organ donor! After the torture, we boarded the helicopter and off we went.

The view was unbelievable! I've never seen such spectacular scenery. I have to admit, though, that I was getting a little panicky because we were in the middle of nowhere. No swimming back if the helicopter went down. They finally set us down on a small floating dock. We boarded a small speed boat to be taken to a luxury multi-level pontoon boat. A roped-off area off one side of the boat was where everyone was snorkeling. Panic was leaving and excitement was arriving!

We went to pick up our snorkeling gear. Next to it was a display of orange Lycra body suits. "What the heck would you want one of those for?" I commented to Laura. It was hot outside, and the body suits were hideous. She didn't have a clue either.

We snorkeled all afternoon and saw everything from clown fish (Nemo!) to a huge napoleon wrasse the size of a dinner table. Amazing!

After hours in the water, it was finally nearing time to leave. Laura and I secured our seats on the cruising boat back to Cairns. We were both hungry, so we ordered potato wedges from the snack bar. In Australia, they are a common restaurant snack, served with sweet Thai chili sauce and sour cream, a tasty combination. While we snacked, an Australian couple sat down next to us. They began chatting to one another about all the fish and coral they had seen. They were surprised that there was no netting around the perimeter of the snorkeling area. Curious, I butted in and asked why there would be a need for netting. To our horror, they described all the poisonous snakes and deadly box jellyfish found in the reef. Apparently the sting of a box jellyfish is so painful that you ultimately die of a heart attack. And *that's* what the Lycra body suits were for. The couple began to fill us in on all the poisonous animals in Australia, but I politely asked them to stop. I prefer to eat my potato wedges with sour cream and sweet Thai chili sauce in blissful ignorance!

Gruyère au Gratin Potatoes

1/4 cup (1/2 stick) butter
1 shallot, minced
1/4 cup all-purpose flour
3 cups milk
1 cup heavy cream
1 1/2 teaspoons salt
1/2 teaspoon white pepper
2 cups (8 ounces) grated Gruyère cheese
1 to 1 1/4 pounds potatoes, peeled and cut into thin slices or bite-size cubes

Preheat the oven to 350 degrees. Melt the butter in a large saucepan. Add the shallot and sauté until tender. Stir in the flour and cook for 1 minute. Stir in the milk and cream. Cook until thick and bubbly. Season with salt and white pepper. Add 1 1/2 cups of the cheese and cook until the cheese is melted, stirring constantly. Add the potatoes and mix gently. Pour into a greased baking dish. Sprinkle with the remaining 1/2 cup cheese. Cover with foil and bake for 30 minutes. Uncover and bake for 10 minutes longer or until the top is light golden brown and the potatoes are tender. Let stand for 5 to 10 minutes before serving.

Makes 6 servings

Garlic and Gouda Mashed Potatoes

2 pounds red potatoes, chopped
1/4 cup (1/2 stick) butter
1/4 cup half-and-half
1 cup (4 ounces) grated Gouda cheese
2 garlic cloves, minced
1/2 teaspoon salt
1/8 teaspoon freshly ground pepper
2 teaspoons chopped fresh parsley

Bring a large saucepan of water to a boil. Add the potatoes. Reduce the heat and simmer, covered, for 20 minutes or until tender; drain. Beat in the butter, half-and-half, cheese, garlic, salt and pepper with an electric mixer. Stir in the parsley and serve immediately.

Makes 6 servings

Sweet Potato Casserole

Sweet Potatoes
3 large sweet potatoes
1/4 cup (1/2 stick) butter
2 eggs
1/2 cup half-and-half or milk
2 tablespoons fresh orange juice
1/4 cup packed dark brown sugar
1 teaspoon grated orange zest
1/2 teaspoon salt
1 teaspoon cinnamon
Pinch of freshly grated nutmeg

Topping
1/2 cup packed light brown sugar
1/4 cup all-purpose flour
1/4 cup (1/2 stick) butter, melted
1/2 cup pecans, chopped
1 teaspoon grated orange zest
Pinch of salt

For the sweet potatoes, preheat the oven to 400 degrees. Pierce each sweet potato three or four times. Place on a baking sheet and bake for 45 minutes or until tender. Let cool slightly. Reduce the oven temperature to 350 degrees. Peel the sweet potatoes. Combine the sweet potatoes with the butter in a large mixing bowl and beat with an electric mixer. Beat in the eggs one at a time. Add the half-and-half, orange juice, brown sugar, orange zest, salt, cinnamon and nutmeg and mix well. Pour into a greased 8×8-inch baking dish.

For the topping, combine the brown sugar, flour, butter, pecans, orange zest and salt in a medium bowl and mix well. Spread evenly over the sweet potatoes. Bake for 30 minutes or until the sweet potatoes are puffed and the topping is golden brown.

Makes 6 servings

Stewed Tomatoes

2 tablespoons butter
1/2 cup chopped onion
2 large ripe tomatoes, chopped
1/4 cup ketchup
1 tablespoon brown sugar
Salt and pepper to taste
1 or 2 slices bread, cut into small pieces

Melt the butter in a medium skillet. Add the onion and sauté until tender. Add the tomatoes and simmer for 10 minutes or until the tomatoes are tender. Add the ketchup, brown sugar, salt and pepper and heat through. Add the bread and mix well. Simmer for 1 to 2 minutes longer and serve immediately.

Makes 4 servings

Oyster Dressing

1/2 cup (1 stick) butter
1 onion, finely chopped
2 ribs celery, finely chopped
1 tablespoon fresh sage, chopped
1 tablespoon fresh thyme, chopped
1 tablespoon flat-leaf parsley, chopped
8 ounces white bread, cut into cubes and dried
2 eggs
3 cups chicken stock
1 pint fresh Willapoint oysters, shucked and drained
Sea salt and freshly cracked pepper to taste

Preheat the oven to 350 degrees. Melt the butter in a medium skillet over medium heat. Add the onion and celery. Sauté for 5 to 8 minutes or until tender. Add the sage, thyme and parsley and sauté for 1 to 2 minutes or until fragrant. Combine the onion mixture with the bread cubes in a large bowl and toss to coat.

Beat the eggs with the stock in a bowl. Add to the bread mixture and stir just until the bread is moistened. Pour into a buttered 9×13-inch glass baking dish and nestle the oysters in the mixture. Cover with foil. Bake for 35 to 40 minutes. Remove the foil and bake for 10 minutes longer or until the dressing is golden brown on top. Let stand for 5 to 10 minutes before serving.

Makes 6 servings

Oysters Down Under

When I was young, my sister Nancy would bring a small pan of oyster dressing to Thanksgiving dinner each year. She would set it next to the regular dressing. After having dissected oysters in biology class, I thought, "Who would eat such a slimy thing?" I never gave oysters another chance, until I found myself at a restaurant in Tasmania.

In medical school in England, I met a third-year resident named Sangeeta from Tasmania. Sangeeta helped me acclimate to the British medical system, and we became friends. We both left England around the same time to continue our medical careers.

By the time I was a third-year resident, I was tired of working 80 to 112 hours a week. I wanted an "away" rotation for a change of scenery for at least a month. International medicine was an acceptable rotation in my residency program, but you had to set up everything yourself. That was okay with me—if there was a way to study while spending a month in a foreign country, I would figure it out.

But where to go? I e-mailed a few scattered friends to catch up, and Sangeeta wrote back to say she was finishing a pediatric rotation in Tasmania and would be happy to help me set up a pediatric rotation. She even said I could stay with her at her new house. Indiana to Tasmania—now that is an "away" rotation. I was so excited!

Once in Tasmania, I met Sangeeta's friend Alex, who is from Zimbabwe by the way. When we were introduced, Alex said, "Now let me get this straight. Are you the American who went to medical school in the Caribbean, trained in England, and is now coming to Tasmania to be taught pediatrics by a Zimbabwean?"

"Yep, that's me!" I replied.

The two weeks in Tasmania were an amazing experience. I learned a lot about pediatrics, and even got to see a Tasmanian devil. Sangeeta had to work a few late shifts, so I tried to get home first and get a decent meal on the table. It seemed like the least I could do, since she was letting me crash at her place. She joked that it was like having a wife!

I had the opportunity to spend some time with her family. When her parents found out I like Indian food, they, being of Indian descent, put together a feast for me. As if that weren't incredible enough, on the last day of my stay, they took me to a restaurant in the harbor of Hobart called Sisco's, where we feasted on seafood. The waiter brought out a huge three-tiered tray of nearly every kind of seafood you could think of. Of course, the tray included oysters on the half shell, and they were by far the biggest oysters I had ever seen. Handing me one, Sangeeta said, "You must try these. They pluck them straight out of the ocean so you can still taste the salty seawater on them, and they are brilliant."

Not wanting to appear rude, I accepted the oyster, thinking "what the heck." I let the oyster slide off into my mouth and down my throat. Oh my gosh! I love oysters! All this time, I had been missing out on these yummy little creatures. That was the end of my thinking oysters were gross. Now I want to put them into everything, not just dressing. Luckily, I've found a partner who loves oysters as much as I do. If it has been a particularly stressful week, we treat ourselves to oysters, prepared in more ways than you can imagine. On really special occasions, we even throw in a glass of Champagne for good measure. It's a great way to de-stress, and as I always say, "Use any excuse to celebrate life."

Three Cheese and Wild Mushroom Risotto

2 tablespoons olive oil
2 tablespoons minced shallot
2 garlic cloves, minced
8 ounces shiitake mushrooms, sliced
8 ounces oyster mushrooms, sliced
8 ounces cremini mushrooms, sliced
1 1/3 cups arborio rice
3 cups chicken broth
1 cup white wine or sherry
2 tablespoons butter
1/4 cup (1 ounce) grated Parmesan cheese
1/4 cup (1 ounce) grated fontina cheese
1/4 cup (1 ounce) grated asiago cheese
2 tablespoons flat-leaf parsley, chopped
Salt and pepper to taste

Heat the olive oil in a medium stockpot. Add the shallot and garlic and sauté just until tender. Add the mushrooms and sauté until tender. Remove the mushroom mixture to a bowl and set aside. Add the rice to the stockpot and cook for 1 to 2 minutes, stirring constatly. Stir in the broth 1 cup at a time. Cook until the liquid is absorbed, stirring constantly. Add the wine and cook until it is absorbed, stirring constantly. Remove from the heat and add the butter, mushroom mixture, Parmesan cheese, fontina cheese, asiago cheese and parsley and mix well. Season with salt and pepper.

Makes 6 servings

Gnocchi with Gorgonzola and Walnuts

1 cup heavy cream
1/4 cup (1/2 stick) butter
4 ounces Gorgonzola cheese, crumbled
Salt to taste
Pinch of freshly grated nutmeg
1 pound gnocchi
1/4 cup chopped walnuts
2 tablespoons freshly grated Parmesan cheese
1 tablespoon fresh parsley, finely chopped

Combine the cream and butter in a medium saucepan. Heat over low heat until the butter is melted. Add the Gorgonzola cheese and cook until melted, stirring constantly. Add salt and the nutmeg and mix well.

Bring a large stockpot of salted water to a boil. Add the gnocchi and boil until they float to the surface. Remove with a slotted spoon and place in a warm serving dish. Add the Gorgonzola cheese mixture and toss to combine. Top with the walnuts, Parmesan cheese and parsley.

Makes 6 servings

White Chocolate Bread Pudding with White Chocolate Brandy Sauce

Chocolate Pots de Crème

Mango White Chocolate Crème Brûlée

Chocolate Fondue

Chocolate Tulip Cups

Triple Berry Crumble Pie

Mango Swirl Key Lime Pie

Tropical Trifle

Tunisian Baklawa

Profiteroles

Very Berry Pizza

Bananas Foster

Cherries Jubilee

Mango and Raspberry Sundaes

Peach Sundaes with Almond Amaretto Sauce

Strawberry Parfaits

Chocolate Mousse

Piña Colada Cheesecake

Banana Rum Cake

Fruit Smoothie

Mint Tea

Gluhwein

Banana Rum

Sangria

Key Lime Martini

Chocolate Martini

Raspberry White Chocolate Martini

Caramel Apple Martini

Pomegranate Mojito

Beverly Hills Iced Tea

Samoan Sling

Berry Cooler

Apricot Brandy Zinger

Thanksgiving Punch

Desserts & Drinks

White Chocolate Bread Pudding with White Chocolate Brandy Sauce

Bread Pudding
16 ounces day-old French bread, torn into bite-size pieces
4 ounces white chocolate, finely chopped
10 eggs
2 egg yolks
3 cups milk
$1^1/_2$ cups sugar
2 teaspoons vanilla bean paste

White Chocolate Brandy Sauce
1 cup heavy cream
$^1/_2$ cup confectioners' sugar
6 tablespoons butter
6 ounces white chocolate, coarsely chopped
3 tablespoons brandy

For the bread pudding, preheat the oven to 400 degrees. Arrange the bread in a 9×13-inch glass baking dish. Sprinkle the white chocolate evenly over the bread. Beat the eggs, egg yolks, milk, sugar and vanilla paste in a large bowl until well mixed. Pour the mixture over the bread, making sure all pieces are soaked. Place the baking dish in a larger baking dish. Add enough hot water to the larger dish to come halfway up the sides of the smaller baking dish. Bake for 30 minutes or until the top is golden brown and center is set. Remove from the water bath; let stand to cool.

For the sauce, heat the cream in the top of a double boiler set over simmering water. Whisk in the confectioners' sugar. Add the butter and heat until melted, whisking constantly. Add the white chocolate several pieces at a time, whisking until melted and blended. Remove from the heat and whisk in the brandy. Spoon the pudding into serving dishes. Top with the sauce. Garnish with grated dark chocolate and fresh strawberries or raspberries.

Makes 10 servings

Chocolate Pots de Crème

2 cups heavy cream
5 ounces bittersweet chocolate, coarsely chopped (preferably Scharffen Berger)
3 egg yolks
1/3 cup packed brown sugar
Dash of salt
1 teaspoon vanilla bean paste

Preheat the oven to 325 degrees. Bring 1 cup of the cream to a boil in a medium saucepan. Remove from the heat. Add the chocolate and whisk until melted and blended. Add the remaining 1 cup cream and whisk to blend. Let stand to cool. Beat the egg yolks, brown sugar and salt in a medium bowl until creamy. Beat in the chocolate mixture gradually. Add the vanilla paste and mix well. Pour the mixture through a fine sieve into a 4-cup glass measure. Arrange ten pots de crème cups in a 9×13-inch baking dish. Pour equal amounts of the chocolate mixture into the cups. Add enough hot water to the baking dish to come halfway up the sides of the cups. Cover the dish with foil. Bake for 25 to 35 minutes or until the edges of the pots de crème are set. Remove the cups from the baking dish. Cover with plastic wrap and chill in the refrigerator for 3 hours or up to 2 days. Serve garnished with whipped cream and chocolate curls.

Makes 10 servings

Note
I first had pots de crème at Chez Gerard, a French restaurant in Covent Garden in London. It was a memorable experience shared among good friends.

Mango White Chocolate Crème Brûlée

2 mangoes, peeled, pitted and diced
5 egg yolks
1/2 cup granulated sugar
2 tablespoons mango liqueur
2 cups heavy cream
4 ounces white chocolate, finely chopped
1 teaspoon vanilla bean paste
1/3 cup packed dark brown sugar
1 tablespoon water

Preheat the oven to 300 degrees. Divide the mangoes evenly among eight ramekins. Beat the egg yolks with 1/4 cup of the granulated sugar and the mango liqueur; set aside. Combine the cream and the remaining 1/4 cup granulated sugar in a medium saucepan. Bring to a simmer. Reduce the heat to low. Add the white chocolate gradually and cook until the chocolate is melted, whisking constantly. Remove from the heat. Add half of the chocolate mixture to the egg yolks in a thin stream, whisking constantly to blend. Pour the mixture into the saucepan and return to the heat. Heat through but do not allow to boil. Remove from the heat and stir in the vanilla paste. Divide the custard evenly among the ramekins. Arrange the ramekins in a glass baking dish. Add enough hot water to the baking dish to come halfway up the sides of the ramekins. Bake for 45 minutes or until the centers are set. Remove the baking dish and let stand for 1 hour. Remove the ramekins from the water and let stand to cool. Chill in the refrigerator for 1 hour or longer.

Preheat the broiler just before serving time. Combine the brown sugar and water in a small bowl. Spoon evenly over the custard. Arrange the ramekins on a baking sheet. Broil for 3 to 5 minutes. Watch closely; do not let the sugar burn. Let stand to cool until the brown sugar hardens.

Makes 8 servings

Chocolate Fondue

1 cup heavy cream
1/3 cup packed dark brown sugar
6 ounces good-quality semisweet chocolate
2 to 4 tablespoons amaretto or Frangelico liqueur
Fruit, cut into bite-size pieces
Angel food cake or pound cake, cut into bite-size pieces
Large marshmallows half-dipped into caramel and rolled in peanuts or toffee bits

Heat the cream and brown sugar in a medium saucepan over medium heat. Cook until the brown sugar is dissolved, stirring constantly. Do not allow the mixture to boil. Remove from the heat. Add the chocolate, whisking until melted and well blended. Stir in the liqueur. Pour into to a fondue pot. Serve with fruit, cake and marshmallows for dipping.

Makes 6 servings

Chocolate Tulip Cups

6 clean helium-grade balloons
6 ounces milk chocolate chips or semisweet chocolate chips
6 tablespoons good-quality raspberry jam
4 cups Chocolate Mousse (page 116)

Rinse and dry the balloons. Blow up the ballons to about a 1-cup volume and secure with a knot. Microwave the chocolate chips in a small deep microwave-safe bowl for 20-second intervals just until melted, stirring between intervals. Do not overheat or the chocolate will seize up. Line a large baking sheet with waxed paper. Dip each balloon into the chocolate, rolling it in four or five directions to make a scallop or tulip petal pattern halfway or more up the balloon on all sides. Set on the waxed paper to dry. Refrigerate for 1 hour to set the chocolate firmly. Create a small hole near the knot in the top of each balloon to let the air out. The balloons should pull away from the chocolate, but you may need to use a wooden pick to facilitate. Discard the balloons.

Spoon the Chocolate Mousse into a pastry bag fitted with a large star tip. Pipe the Mousse into the chocolate cups until one-third full. Spoon 1 tablespoon of the jam into the center of the mousse in each cup. Pipe enough additional Chocolate Mousse over the jam to make the cups two-thirds full. Garnish with fresh raspberries and fresh mint. Chill until serving time.

Makes 6 servings

Triple Berry Crumble Pie

Berry Pie
2 cups fresh or frozen blackberries
2 cups fresh or frozen blueberries
1 cup fresh or frozen raspberries
1 1/2 cups sugar
1/2 cup all-purpose flour
Dash of salt
1 frozen (9-inch) deep-dish pie shell

Crumble Topping
1/2 cup all-purpose flour
1/2 cup oats
1/2 cup packed dark brown sugar
6 tablespoons butter, softened
1/2 teaspoon cinnamon
1/8 teaspoon freshly grated nutmeg
1/4 teaspoon salt

For the pie, preheat the oven to 400 degrees. Combine the blackberries, blueberries and raspberries in a large bowl. Combine the sugar, flour and salt in a medium bowl. Pour the sugar mixture over the berries. Toss gently to coat the berries. Place the pie shell on a baking sheet. Spread the berries evenly in the pie shell. Wrap the edge of the pie shell with foil.

For the topping, combine the flour, oats, brown sugar, butter, cinnamon, nutmeg and salt in a medium bowl. Mix with a fork until crumbly. Spread over the berries. Bake for 40 to 55 minutes or until the topping is golden brown and the juices are thickened. Remove the foil from the edge for the last 15 minutes of baking. Let stand to cool completely before slicing.

Makes 8 servings

Mango Swirl Key Lime Pie

Coconut Crust

1 cup fine graham cracker crumbs
3/4 cup sweetened shredded coconut
6 tablespoons butter, melted
1/4 cup packed dark brown sugar

Filling

4 egg yolks
1 tablespoon lime zest
1/2 cup Key lime juice (3 to 6 Key limes)
1 (14-ounce) can sweetened condensed milk
1 ripe mango, peeled and chopped

For the crust, preheat the oven to 325 degrees. Combine the graham cracker crumbs with the coconut in a bowl. Add the butter and brown sugar and mix well. Press the mixture evenly over the bottom and up the side of a 9-inch pie plate. Bake for 15 to 17 minutes or until light brown. Let stand for 20 minutes or until cool.

For the filling, beat the egg yolks and lime zest in a bowl. Add the lime juice and whisk to blend. Let stand for 15 minutes to thicken. Add the condensed milk and mix well. Purée the mango pulp; press through a sieve into a bowl. Spoon the filling into the piecrust. Spoon the mango purée into a pastry bag fitted with a small plain tip. Pipe a pinwheel beginning in the center of the pie filling and proceeding to the outer edge near the crust. Use a knife to slice down and through the filling to distribute the mango throughout. Bake for 15 to 17 minutes or until the center is set but still has a slight jiggle. Let stand to cool for 20 to 30 minutes. Chill for 3 hours or longer. Garnish with whipped cream and a slice of lime.

Makes 6 servings

Tropical Trifle

8 ounces cream cheese, softened
1 (14-ounce) can sweetened condensed milk
1 (15-ounce) can cream of coconut
1 (10-inch) angel food cake, torn into bite-size pieces
1 small pineapple, cut into bite-size pieces
2 ripe mangoes, cut into bite-size pieces
2 bananas, cut into 1/4-inch slices
1 (11-ounce) can mandarin oranges, drained
8 ounces whipped topping, or 1 cup heavy whipping cream, whipped

Beat the cream cheese in a bowl with an electric mixer until fluffy. Add the condensed milk and cream of coconut and mix well. Layer half the cake, half the cream cheese mixture, half the fruit and half the whipped topping in a trifle bowl. Repeat the layers with the remaining ingredients. Garnish with fresh pineapple or mandarin oranges. Chill in the refrigerator for 1 hour or longer before serving.

Makes 12 servings

"Hey, Laura...Let's Hop on Our Camels and Go Pick Up Some Baklawa!"

One of the most memorable events of my third year of medical school in England was attending a doctor's ball at Leed's Castle. As exciting as it was, the events leading up to the evening were even more exciting.

On our commute to a psychiatry rotation in London, Laura and I passed the same billboard every day: a woman lounging on the beach beside pristine turquoise water. It was an advertisement for tourism to Tunisia. One gloomy morning six months into our stay, it was just too inviting for Laura to pass up. "Let's go there and get a tan for the ball," she said.

She was serious about that tan, and when we investigated, we found that flights and hotels were surprisingly reasonably priced. The hotel she found on the Internet showed a picture of someone riding a camel on the beach—it was as if it were calling directly to us. We proceeded to book our trip in a frenzy. We were going to be tan and rested for the ball.

Normally, I like to research where I'm going for vacation, but there was no time for that with our hectic rotations. So even after arriving in Tunis, the capital, I knew nothing about Tunisia except you could ride camels and get a tan. We were both surprised to see that everything in the airport was written in Arabic. Hmm. We hadn't known Tunisia was an Arabic country.

After a white-knuckle cab ride, we arrived at our hotel. I plopped on the bed while Laura headed to the bathroom. I turned on the television and flipped through the channels to check out Tunisian television. The weather channel featured a big map of Tunisia and surrounding countries. My eyes nearly popped out of my head. "Laura!" I exclaimed. "Get out here! Did you know Tunisia is in between Libya and Algeria?"

"What?" she yelled, running out of the bathroom. She took one look at the map and said, "Holy crap!" Little did we know Tunisia is a very small country nestled between very large Algeria and Libya! I know what you are thinking. Pretty scary that two prospective physicians could be so dumb!

Once the shock wore off, we visited the concierge to book a camel ride for the next day. After all, we had a tan to get and camels to ride, even if it meant getting kidnapped by terrorists in the process. Next, we set off to the beach to work on our tans, which helped wash away our tensions.

The following day we left the hotel to pursue our camel riding adventure. We arrived at the stable and picked our camels. We struggled to mount the awkward animals and set off to ride them into the Sahara Desert. Reality hit us and we were laughing like two schoolgirls. "Laura!" I exclaimed. "We're on camels in the Sahara Desert!"

"I know!" she drawled in her southern accent.

We ascended a hill and were admiring the magnificent view when suddenly we stopped at the peak. The guide, who spoke very little English, motioned for us to get down off the camels. "A bit odd," I thought. Others with us were dismounting so we complied and dismounted our camels. We were led down the side of a hill spotted with hutlike dwellings. As we were hiking down the hill, I turned to Laura and jokingly commented, "Hey, Laura, I think this is about the time we get sold into slavery."

"That's not funny!" she fumed.

Once we had been led into a hut, native Tunisians greeted us with big smiles and draped us in traditional Tunisian garb. Tunisian music played. We were encouraged to dance and were fed baklawa (baklava) and mint tea. Laura and I laughed and danced, relieved that there were no signs of slave trading. The baklawa was so flaky and delicious and the mint tea was refreshing.

We made our way back to our camels and then to the stables safe and sound. We spent our remaining time in Tunisia working on our tans for the ball. We had accomplished our goal and had an unbelievable adventure to remember for the rest of our lives!

Tunisian Baklawa

Syrup
1 cup sugar
1 cup water
1/2 cup honey
2 tablespoons lemon juice
1 teaspoon vanilla extract

Baklawa
2 cups walnuts, chopped
1 cup pistachios, chopped
1 cup almonds, chopped
1/4 cup granulated sugar
1/4 cup packed brown sugar
1 teaspoon cinnamon
1 (16-ounce) package frozen phyllo dough, thawed in the package
2 cups (4 sticks) butter, melted

For the syrup, combine the sugar and water in a medium saucepan. Cook for 10 to 15 minutes or until the sugar is dissolved and the liquid is thickened to a syrupy consistency, stirring constantly. Stir in the honey, lemon juice and vanilla. Let stand for 10 to 15 minutes to cool.

For the baklawa, preheat the oven to 350 degrees. Toss the walnuts, pistachios, almonds, granulated sugar, brown sugar and cinnamon in a large bowl. Unroll the phyllo dough. Cover with waxed paper topped with a damp kitchen towel. Layer a sheet of dough in a greased 9×13-inch baking pan, cutting to size if needed. Brush with the butter. Repeat with seven layers of dough, recovering the unused the dough each time. Spread half of the walnut mixture over the dough. Layer with eight phyllo sheets, brushing each with butter. Spread the remaining walnut mixture over the phyllo. Layer with eight phyllo sheets, brushing each with butter. Score the top half of the baklawa into diamond shapes with a sharp knife. Bake for 45 to 50 minutes or until golden brown. Pour the syrup over the baklawa. Let stand for 4 hours or until the syrup is absorbed and the baklawa is cool.

Makes 8 servings

Note
In Tunisia, baklava is spelled with a "w"—baklawa. No matter how you spell it, it is delicious!

Profiteroles

Cream Puffs
1/4 cup (1/2 stick) butter
1 cup water
1 cup all-purpose flour
1/4 teaspoon salt
4 eggs

Chocolate Sauce
1 1/2 cups heavy cream
3/4 cup packed dark brown sugar
7 ounces bittersweet chocolate, chopped (preferably Scharffen Berger or Valrhona)
1/4 cup (1/2 stick) butter
2 teaspoons vanilla extract

Filling
1 pint vanilla ice cream
1 pint dulce de leche ice cream
1 pint coffee ice cream

For the cream puffs, preheat the oven to 350 degrees. Bring the butter and water to a boil in a medium saucepan. Remove from the heat. Add the flour and salt all at once. Beat vigorously with a wooden spoon until the mixture forms a ball. Beat in the eggs one at a time until the mixture is smooth and satiny. Drop the dough by tablespoonfuls onto an ungreased baking sheet to make twenty-four small mounds. Bake for 30 minutes or until golden brown. Let stand to cool.

For the chocolate sauce, heat the cream in a medium saucepan over medium heat. Add the brown sugar and cook until the sugar is dissolved, stirring constantly. Remove from the heat and add the chocolate. Stir until the chocolate is melted and well blended. Add the butter and vanilla and stir to blend.

For the filling, remove the tops and doughy centers of the puffs. Fill eight of the puffs with vanilla ice cream, eight with dulce de leche ice cream and the remaining eight with coffee ice cream. For each serving, arrange three puffs on a plate, each with a different flavor ice cream. Top with chocolate sauce.

Makes 8 servings

Very Berry Pizza

Crust
$1^1/_2$ cups all-purpose flour
1 cup (2 sticks) butter
$^1/_4$ cup packed brown sugar
$^1/_4$ cup chopped pecans

Filling
8 ounces cream cheese, softened
$^3/_4$ cup confectioners' sugar
8 ounces whipped topping

Topping
1 (3-ounce) package strawberry gelatin
$^1/_2$ cup sugar
Dash of salt
$^1/_4$ cup cornstarch
1 cup water
1 cup blueberries
1 cup sliced strawberries
1 cup blackberries
1 cup raspberries

For the crust, preheat the oven to 400 degrees. Combine the flour, butter, brown sugar and pecans in a large bowl to form a dough. Spread the dough evenly in a 16-inch pizza pan. Bake for 10 to 15 minutes. Let stand to cool.

For the filling, beat the cream cheese and confectioners' sugar in a bowl with an electric mixer until smooth. Fold in the whipped topping. Spread the mixture over the crust.

For the topping, whisk the gelatin, sugar, salt and cornstarch in a medium saucepan. Whisk in the water. Cook over medium heat for 7 minutes or until bubbly and thickened. Let cool slightly. Add the berries and stir gently to coat. Spread over the filling. Chill for 3 hours or longer before serving.

Makes 8 servings

Bananas Foster

1/2 stick (1/4 cup) butter
1/2 cup packed dark brown sugar
2 tablespoons heavy cream
4 firm bananas, cut into halves and sliced lengthwise
1/4 cup dark rum
1 pint vanilla ice cream, scooped into four dishes

Melt the butter in a medium skillet. Add the brown sugar and cook until dissolved, stirring constantly. Stir in the cream. Add the sliced bananas. Cook until the bananas are slightly softened. Add the rum. Remove from the heat and quickly ignite with a long match. When the flame subsides, spoon the bananas and sauce over the ice cream. Serve immediately.

Makes 4 servings

Cherries Jubilee

2 (16-ounce) cans dark cherries
1/4 cup Triple Sec
1/2 cup cherry-flavored brandy
1/4 cup sugar
1 1/2 tablespoons cornstarch
1/4 cup brandy
Vanilla bean ice cream

Drain the cherries, reserving 1/2 cup of the liquid. Combine the cherries, Triple Sec and 1/2 cup brandy in a bowl. Chill in the refrigerator for 48 hours. Combine the sugar and cornstarch in a small bowl. Add the reserved liquid and stir until the cornstarch is dissolved. Combine with the cherry mixture in a small saucepan. Cook over medium heat until the liquid is thickened and bubbly. Pour into a chafing dish. To serve, pour 1/4 cup brandy into a metal ladle. Ignite with a long match or grill lighter. Quickly pour the brandy over the cherry mixture. Stir the flaming brandy into the cherry mixture until the flame subsides. Spoon the cherry mixture over the ice cream. Serve immediately.

Makes 6 servings

Mango and Raspberry Sundaes

1 pint raspberries
1/4 cup simple syrup
1 large mango
1 pint vanilla ice cream

Combine the raspberries and 2 tablespoons of the simple syrup in a food processor. Process until puréed. Pour into a small dish; set aside. Clean the food processor. Combine the mango and remaining 2 tablespoons simple syrup in the food processor. Arrange two scoops of ice cream in each of four dishes. Spoon raspberry purée over one of the scoops and mango purée over the other. Garnish with fresh mint. Serve with chocolate or dulce de leche pirouette cookies. Serve immediately.

Makes 4 servings

Peach Sundaes with Almond Amaretto Sauce

1/4 cup (1/2 stick) butter
1/2 cup packed brown sugar
2 tablespoons heavy cream
6 peaches, peeled and sliced
1/4 cup amaretto
Vanilla ice cream
1/4 cup sliced almonds

Melt the butter in a medium saucepan over medium heat. Add the brown sugar and cook until the brown sugar is dissolved and the mixture is bubbly, stirring constantly. Stir in the cream and peaches. Reduce the heat to medium-low and cook until the peaches are tender, stirring occasionally. Stir in the amaretto. Cook for 1 to 2 minutes longer. Let stand to cool slightly. Scoop the ice cream into six bowls. Spoon equal amounts of the peaches and sauce over the ice cream. Sprinkle with the almonds. Serve immediately.

Makes 6 servings

Strawberry Parfaits

1 cup sour cream
1/4 cup packed brown sugar
1/2 cup whipped topping
1/4 cup Cointreau
2 cups fresh strawberries, sliced
4 slices angel food cake, cut into cubes

Combine the sour cream and brown sugar in a small bowl. Stir until the brown sugar is dissolved. Fold in the whipped topping and 2 tablespoons of the Cointreau. Toss the strawberries and the remaining 2 tablespoons Cointreau in another bowl. Reserve four strawberry slices for the topping. Layer the cake, strawberries and sour cream mixture one-half at a time in four parfait glasses. Top each with one of the reserved strawberry slices. Garnish with fresh mint.

Makes 4 servings

Note

For a low-fat version of this recipe, use low-fat or nonfat sour cream and nonfat whipped topping.

Chocolate Mousse

3 egg yolks
2 tablespoons sugar
6 ounces good-quality semisweet chocolate, finely chopped
3 tablespoons butter
2 to 4 tablespoons Chambord, Grand Marnier or brandy
3 egg whites
2 tablespoons sugar
¾ cup heavy whipping cream
2 tablespoons sugar

Whisk the egg yolks and 2 tablespoons sugar in the top of a double boiler set over simmering water until the sugar is dissolved. Remove from the heat and stir in the chocolate and butter. Stir until both are melted and well blended. Stir in the liqueur. Let stand to cool.

Beat the egg whites in a mixing bowl until soft peaks form. Add 2 tablespoons sugar gradually, beating until stiff peaks form. Set aside.

Beat the whipping cream in a mixing bowl until soft peaks form. Sprinkle with 2 tablespoons sugar and beat just until blended.

Fold the chocolate mixture gradually into the beaten egg whites. Fold in the whipped cream gradually. Spoon into dessert cups or chocolate shells. Chill in the refrigerator until set.

Makes 6 servings

Note
This recipe can be prepared a day ahead and chilled until serving time.

Piña Colada Cheesecake

Macaroon Crust
1/4 cup (1/2 stick) butter, softened
20 macaroon cookies, crushed

Filling
24 ounces cream cheese, softened
3/4 cup packed brown sugar
2 tablespoons cornstarch
4 eggs
2/3 cup canned crushed pineapple, drained
6 tablespoons coconut rum
2 teaspoons vanilla extract

Coconut Sauce
1 can cream of coconut
3 tablespoons coconut rum
2 tablespoons light rum

For the crust, preheat the oven to 350 degrees. Combine the butter and cookies in a medium bowl and mix well. Press the mixture over the bottom of a baking parchment-lined 9-inch springform pan. Wrap the bottom of the pan with heavy-duty foil.

For the filling, beat the cream cheese, brown sugar and cornstarch in a large bowl. Add the eggs one at a time and mix well. Beat in the pineapple, coconut rum and vanilla. Pour the mixture into the crust. Place the springform pan in a larger pan. Add enough hot water to the larger pan to come halfway up the side of the springform pan. Bake for 15 minutes. Reduce the oven temperature to 225 degrees and bake for 1 hour longer or until the center no longer looks shiny. Run a knife around the edge to loosen the cheesecake from the pan. Chill until cooled and firmly set.

For the sauce, combine the cream of coconut, coconut rum and the light rum in a small saucepan. Heat just until warm. Pour over the cheesecake to serve. Garnish with fresh pineapple.

Makes 12 servings

Banana Rum Cake

Cake

½ cup (1 stick) butter, softened
1 cup granulated sugar
1/3 cup packed dark brown sugar
3 eggs
2 cups all-purpose flour
1 (3-ounce) package vanilla instant pudding mix
2 teaspoons baking powder
1 teaspoon baking soda
½ teaspoon salt
¾ cup buttermilk
1 cup mashed banana
1 1/2 teaspoons vanilla extract
1/2 cup chopped pecans

Banana Rum Glaze

1/4 cup (1/2 stick) butter
1/4 cup granulated sugar
1/4 cup packed dark brown sugar
2 tablespoons water
1/4 cup banana-flavored rum
1/2 cup prepared cream cheese frosting

For the cake, preheat the oven to 325 degrees. Beat the butter, granulated sugar and brown sugar in a large bowl until light and fluffy. Add the eggs one at a time and beat until slightly fluffy. Combine the flour, pudding mix, baking powder, baking soda and salt in another bowl. Add to the butter mixture alternately with the buttermilk, mixing well after each addition. Stir in the banana and vanilla.

Grease and flour a bundt pan. Sprinkle the pecans over the bottom of the pan. Pour the batter into the pan and smooth the top. Bake for 55 to 60 minutes or until the cake tests done. Cool in the pan for 10 minutes. Invert onto a platter.

For the glaze, melt the butter in a small saucepan. Add the granulated sugar, brown sugar and water. Cook for 5 minutes or until the sugar is melted. Remove from the heat and add the rum. Poke holes in the top of the cake and brush with the rum mixture. Microwave the cream cheese frosting for 10 seconds on High or until it reaches a pouring consistency. Drizzle the frosting over the cake. Allow to cool completely before serving.

Makes 12 servings

Fruit Smoothie

1 kiwifruit
½ banana
3 large strawberries
6 ounces vanilla yogurt
4 ice cubes
1 tablespoon flax seed, finely ground (optional)
1 scoop of soy protein powder (optional)
Milk (optional)

Combine the kiwifruit, banana, strawberries, yogurt, ice cubes, flax seed and protein powder in a blender container. Process until smooth. Thin with a small amount of milk if needed. Pour into a tall glass and garnish with a fresh strawberry.

Makes 1 serving

Mint Tea

4 cups water
4 green tea bags
1/2 cup fresh spearmint leaves
1/2 cup sugar

Bring the water to a boil in a medium saucepan. Turn off the heat and add the tea bags. Let steep for 6 to 10 minutes. Discard the tea bags. Place the spearmint and sugar in a teapot. Add the tea. Let steep for 5 minutes longer. Stir to dissolve the sugar. Serve hot.

Makes 3 to 4 servings

Gluhwein

1 (750-milliliter) bottle full-bodied red wine, such as merlot or burgundy
1/4 cup brandy
1/2 cup sugar
4 cinnamon sticks
6 whole cloves
4 allspice berries
4 orange slices
2 lemon slices

Combine the wine, brandy, sugar, cinnamon sticks, cloves, allspice, orange slices and lemon slices in a large saucepan. Heat over low heat for 1 hour; do not let the mixture boil. Serve warm in mugs garnished with orange slices and cinnamon sticks.

Makes 4 servings

More Gluhwein! I Need More Gluhwein!

I first had gluhwein on a ski trip to the French Alps during my third year of medical school. I was studying in England, and over Easter weekend, many of the American students were returning to the United States to visit family. My friend Clay and I were trying to conserve money, so I talked him into going on a "budget" ski trip to the Alps instead. Clay had skied before, so he could teach me, he said. This was my first mistake.

The fifteen-hour bus ride ended in Albertville, France. The next day, I learned the most important lesson: how to stop. After an hour, I felt I had mastered the "snow plow." I was ready for a small slope. Conditions weren't ideal. As it was warming up, melting snow left grassy patches. After a few runs, we were weary and left.

On our second day, we warmed up on the little slope, and then decided to move on to a more challenging grade. Clay read the map and led the way. My second mistake. We arrived at the top of the hill, which seemed to take a long, long time, and we started down. The slope seemed much more challenging than I expected. I quickly discovered that Clay had read the map wrong and we were on a "blue" slope! Did I mention that we were in the Alps? I would begin skiing but would gain so much speed that I couldn't slow down. So I worked on my falling technique. When I tired of skiing, I just sat down. I thought I had mastered falling. My third major mistake.

Clay was doing really well, so he decided to ski down and wait for me. I figured he just didn't want to watch me kill myself. I was determined to "just go for it." I headed down, making sure I was swishing back and forth in wide swaths to control my speed. I was doing well until I reached the part of the mountain with snowless patches. I panicked and began making much smaller turns, thereby picking up great speed. I was thinking about using my sitting-down technique when POW! I lost control and flipped head-over-ski boots three times! My skis, glasses, scarf, and hat went flying. I even lost my poles. A couple of concerned skiers approached my twisted body and asked whether I was okay, adding, "That was spectacular!" I was still on my back when Clay found me, and I was laughing so hard I was crying. I eventually picked myself up and gathered my stuff, slowly making my way down the rest of the mountain. We took a break at the lodge and warmed up with a nice mug of gluhwein (mulled wine) before returning to the mountain. My hand had begun to hurt, though the wine was helping to numb it . . . and the rest of me.

By the next morning, my hand was black and blue. I knew it was injured, but I didn't want to miss the final day of skiing, particularly since a fresh layer of powdery snow had fallen overnight. Clay found tape at a pharmacy and wrapped my hand and thumb. After three runs, it was apparent that I was protecting my hand. I returned to wait at the lodge and drink gluhwein while Clay had a few more ski runs.

We made it back to England and the emergency room. No broken bones but a torn ligament, coincidentally known as "skier's thumb," did require surgery. Even more odd, the hand surgeon had trained in the U.S. and had been to my hometown for a conference. It's a small world!

Banana Rum

2 cups water
2 cups sugar
1 (750-milliliter) bottle good-quality rum or spiced rum
1 ripe banana

Bring the water and sugar to a boil in a medium saucepan. Boil for 2 minutes or until the sugar is completely dissolved. Let stand to cool completely. Pour the rum into a clean dry glass container or bottle. Cut the banana into halves crosswise and then into quarters lengthwise. Add to the rum. Add the simple syrup. Refrigerate for 1 to 2 weeks to infuse.

Makes 12 servings

Note
On the French side of the Caribbean island of St. Martin, it is common after a meal for banana rum served in shot glasses to make the rounds. It's the perfect way to finish off a meal!

Sangria

1/2 cup water
1/2 cup sugar
1/2 cup brandy
2 (750-milliliter) bottles rioja wine
2 lemons, sliced
2 navel orange, sliced
2 limes, sliced
1 cup fresh pineapple chunks
3 or 4 cinnamon sticks

Bring the water and sugar to a boil in a medium saucepan. Boil for 2 minutes or until the sugar is completely dissolved. Let stand to cool completely. Combine the simple syrup, brandy, wine, lemons, oranges, limes, pineapple and cinnamon sticks in a large pitcher. Let stand for 6 to 8 hours or longer before serving.

Makes 8 servings

Key Lime Martini

2 ounces vanilla vodka
1 ounce Licor 43
1 ounce Key lime syrup (half Key lime juice and half simple syrup)
1/2 ounce Midori melon liqueur
2 ounces heavy cream
Crushed graham cracker crumbs

Combine the vodka, Licor 43, Key lime syrup, melon liqueur and cream with ice in a cocktail shaker. Shake well to blend. Dip the rim of a martini glass into water and then into crushed graham cracker crumbs. Pour the drink into the glass. Garnish with a lime slice.

Makes 1 serving

Chocolate Martini

2 ounces vanilla vodka
1 ounce chocolate liqueur
1/2 ounce chocolate syrup
2 ounces half-and-half
Finely grated chocolate

Combine the vodka, chocolate liqueur, chocolate syrup and half-and-half with ice in a cocktail shaker. Shake well to blend. Dip the rim of a martini glass into water and then into finely grated chocolate. Pour the drink into the glass. Garnish by floating a chocolate kiss in the drink and placing a chocolate-dipped strawberry on the rim.

Makes 1 serving

Raspberry White Chocolate Martini

1 ounce Ghirardelli white chocolate sauce
1/2 ounce vanilla vodka
1/2 ounce vodka
1/2 ounce Chambord

Combine the white chocolate sauce, vanilla vodka and vodka with ice in a cocktail shaker. Shake well to blend. Pour into a martini glass. Pour the Chambord down one side of the drink so it sinks to the bottom. Garnish with three raspberries skewered on a swizzle stick.

Makes 1 serving

Caramel Apple Martini

2 ounces apple-flavored schnapps or vodka
1 ounce butterscotch-flavored schnapps
1 ounce vanilla vodka
Caramel ice cream topping

Combine the apple-flavored schnapps, butterscotch-flavored schnapps and vanilla vodka with ice in a cocktail shaker. Shake well to blend. Drizzle caramel topping over the bottom of a martini glass. Pour the drink into the glass. Garnish with a slice of green apple and a vanilla caramel skewered on a swizzle stick.

Makes 1 serving

Pomegranate Mojito

1 ounce pomegranate liqueur
1 1/2 ounces white rum
2 ounces pomegranate juice
1 ounce fresh lime juice
2 tablespoons simple syrup
1 lime wedge
4 or 5 fresh mint leaves
Club soda
1 tablespoon pomegranate seeds

Combine the liqueur, rum, pomegranate juice, lime juice and simple syrup with ice in a cocktail shaker. Shake well to blend. Muddle the lime and mint in a tall glass. Fill the glass with ice. Pour the drink over the ice. Top with club soda and the pomegranate seeds. Garnish additional mint.

Makes 1 drink

Beverly Hills Iced Tea

1 1/2 ounces vodka
1 1/2 ounces rum
1 1/2 ounces gin
1 1/2 ounces tequila
1 1/2 ounces Triple Sec
4 ounces fresh lemon juice
4 ounces simple syrup
6 ounces dry sparkling wine or Champagne

Mix the vodka, rum, gin, tequila, Triple Sec, lemon juice and simple syrup with ice in a cocktail shaker. Shake well to blend. Pour into two large fishbowl-type glasses filled with ice. Top each drink with 3 ounces of the wine. Float a lemon slice in each drink. Serve immediately.

Makes 2 servings

Samoan Sling

2 ounces lychee-flavored liqueur or lychee juice
1 ounce blue curaçao
1 ounce vodka
Club soda
1 ounce grenadine

Fill a 12-ounce highball glass with ice. Pour the lychee-flavored liqueur, curaçao and vodka over the ice. Top with club soda and stir to blend. Pour the grenadine down the side of the glass so it sinks to the bottom. Garnish with a maraschino cherry and a lychee skewered on a swizzle stick.

Makes 1 drink

Note
I had a drink similar to this while visiting a friend in New Zealand. I loved it so much that I made her take me to three different liquor stores to find a bottle of the lychee-flavored liqueur to bring home. It's hard to find but so worth the effort. If you can't find lychee-flavored liqueur, lychee juice can be found at Asian grocery stores.

Berry Cooler

4 raspberries
4 blackberries
6 blueberries
3 or 4 fresh mint leaves
1 lime wedge
2 ounces vodka
3 ounces grapefruit juice
3 ounces lemon-lime soda

Muddle the berries, mint and lime in a tall highball glass. Fill the glass with ice. Add the vodka, grapefruit juice and soda and stir to blend. Serve with a straw. Garnish with fresh mint and a lime wedge on the rim.

Makes 1 drink

Apricot Brandy Zinger

4 ounces apricot nectar
2 ounces brandy
3 ounces club soda
1/2 ounce grenadine

Fill an old-fashioned glass with crushed ice. Add the apricot nectar, brandy and club soda and stir gently to blend. Pour the grenadine down the side of the glass so it sinks to the bottom. Garnish with a maraschino cherry.

Makes 1 drink

Thanksgiving Punch

6 ounces raspberry vodka
2 ounces Triple Sec
12 ounces orange juice
12 ounces cranberry juice
1/2 cup frozen pink lemonade concentrate, thawed
1/4 cup frozen limeade concentrate, thawed
1 (750-milliliter) bottle dry sparkling white wine, chilled
1 pint berry sherbet
Fresh orange slices
Fresh lime slices
1 pint fresh or frozen raspberries

Combine the vodka, Triple Sec, orange juice, cranberry juice, lemonade concentrate and limeade concentrate in a punch bowl and mix well. Add the wine. Add scoops of the sherbet. Float the orange slices, lime slices and raspberries in the punch. Garnish with mint sprigs.

Makes 6 servings

Note
If serving this at an event that includes children, leave out the alcohol; add an extra cup of juice, and substitute citrus soda for the sparkling wine.

General Wine and Food Pairing Guide

FOOD	WHITE WINE	RED WINE
Chicken	Chardonnay, Sauvignon Blanc, Viognier	Pinot Noir, Beaujolais, Burgundy
Turkey	Sauvignon Blanc	
Game Birds		Pinot Noir, Merlot, Zinfandel, Rioja, Malbec, Shiraz, Cabernet Sauvignon
Duck	Chardonnay, Reisling, Viognier	Pinot Noir, Zinfandel, Rioja, Valpolicella
Pork	Chardonnay	Pinot Noir, Zinfandel, Merlot, Rioja, Malbec, Shiraz, Chianti, Cabernet Sauvignon
Veal	Chardonnay	Pinot Noir, Zinfandel, Merlot, Rioja, Malbec, Shiraz, Chianti, Cabernet Sauvignon
Beef		Pinot Noir, Cabernet Sauvignon, Merlot, Zinfandel, Shiraz, Malbec
Lamb		Bordeaux, Cabernet Sauvignon, Merlot, Zinfandel, Shiraz, Malbec
Venison/Game Meats		Zinfandel, Cabernet Sauvignon, Shiraz, Malbec
Oysters	Champagne, Sauvignon Blanc, Reisling	
Scallops/Shrimp/Crab	Sancerre, Sauvignon Blanc, Chardonnay, Gewürztraminer	
Calamari	Sauvignon Blanc, Chardonnay, Reisling, Gewürztraminer	
Lobster	Chardonnay, Viognier	
Snapper/Halibut	Sauvignon Blanc, Chardonnay	

Food	White Wine	Red Wine
Orange Roughy		Pinot Noir
Salmon/Tuna/ Swordfish	Chardonnay, Viognier	Pinot Noir, Merlot, Syrah, Rioja, Valpolicella
Sushi/Sashimi	Champagne, Reisling, Gewürztraminer, Saki	
Pasta with Cream Sauce	Chardonnay, Sauvignon Blanc, Pinot Grigio, Viognier	Pinot Noir
Pasta with Pesto	Sauvignon Blanc	Pinot Noir, Zinfandel
Pasta with Red Sauce		Zinfandel, Chianti, Cabernet Sauvignon, Merlot, Sangiovese, Syrah
Pizza	Sauvignon Blanc	Merlot, Sangiovese, Zinfandel
Mexican	White Zinfandel	Zinfandel
Indian	Gewürztraminer, Riesling	Zinfandel, Syrah
Japanese	Sancerre, Champagne, Sauvignon Blanc	
Chinese	Gewürztraminer, Riesling	Merlot
Thai	Chardonnay, Gewürztraminer, Riesling	Zinfandel
Brie/Camembert	Chardonnay, Gewürztraminer, Riesling	Pinot Noir, Burgundy, Zinfandel
Goat Cheese/Feta	Sauvignon Blanc, Sancerre, Pouilly-Fume	Zinfandel
Fontina/Edam/ Gouda/Havarti	Chardonnay, Gewürztraminer, Riesling	Pinot Noir, Zinfandel, Merlot
Blue Cheese/ Gorgonzola	Sauternes	Cabernet Sauvignon, Zinfandel, Shiraz, Madeira, Port
Parmesan/Romano/ Asiago	Chardonnay	Merlot, Zinfandel, Cabernet Sauvignon, Shiraz
Cheddar	Chardonnay	Shiraz, Zinfandel, Merlot
Smoked Cheese	Gewürztraminer, Riesling, Sauternes	Shiraz

Suggested Wine and Food Pairings for Select Recipes

Food	White Wine	Red Wine
Nigiri Sushi	Champagne/sparkling wine, Sauvignon Blanc, Gewürztraminer, Riesling	
Crab-Stuffed Mushrooms	Chardonnay, Sauvignon Blanc	Pinot Noir
Stuffed Grilled Eggplant	Pouilly-Fume	Zinfandel
Proscuitto-Wrapped Scallops	Chardonnay, Sauvignon Blanc	Pinot Noir
Tuscan Bean Dip	Sauvignon Blanc	Pinot Noir, Zinfandel
Yin Yang Shrimp	Gewürztraminer, Riesling	
Calamari with Sweet Thai Chili Sauce	Gewürztraminer, Riesling	Pinot Noir
Lemon Pepper Fried Oysters	Champagne/sparkling wine, Sauvignon Blanc	
Spinach and Artichoke Dip	Viognier, Pinot Grigio	
Dolmas		Pinot Noir, Merlot, Zinfandel
Rumaki		Zinfandel
Crab Eggs Benedict	Champagne/sparkling wine, Mimosa	
Spanish Quiche	Rioja	
Shrimp Scampi and Bacon Pizza on the Grill	Chardonnay, Sauvignon Blanc	
Oyster Po' Boys	Sauvignon Blanc	
Roast Chicken, Red Pepper and Havarti Pitas		Zinfandel
Duck Breast Sandwiches		Pinot Noir, Merlot, Zinfandel

Food	White Wine	Red Wine
Croque Monsieur	Chardonnay, Sauvignon Blanc	
Italian Steak Panini		Zinfandel, Cabernet Sauvignon, Merlot, Shiraz
Coconut Curry Pumpkin Soup	Viognier, Gewürztraminer, Riesling	
Lobster Bisque	Unoaked Chardonnay, Pinot Grigio	Pinot Noir, Zinfandel
Monterey Blend Mushroom Soup		Pinot Noir
French Onion Soup		Merlot, Zinfandel
Seafood Chowder	Chardonnay, Pinot Gris	
Hearty Split Pea Soup	Sauvignon Blanc	
Coronation Chicken Salad	Gewürztraminer, Riesling	
Beef Wellington		Pinot Noir, Zinfandel
Cedar Plank Salmon Steaks in Asian Marinade		Pinot Noir
Spanish Paella		Rioja
Sesame Seared Ahi Tuna Steaks	Gewürztraminer, Reisling	Pinot Noir
Pork Chops Stuffed with Smoked Gouda and Apple		Zinfandel, Shiraz, Merlot
Barbecue Boston Butt		Zinfandel, Shiraz
Armenian Shish Kabobs		Zinfandel, Merlot, Shiraz, Cabernet Sauvignon
Smoked Peking Duck		Pinot Noir
Hearty Black Bean Burritos		Zinfandel, Malbec

Food	White Wine	Red Wine
Cheesy Chicken and Portobello Lasagna	Chardonnay, Pinot Grigio, Viognier	Pinot Noir
Pasta Sfoglia Pollo con Spinaci		Pinot Noir, Zinfandel
Roasted Vegetable Medley		Zinfandel, Shiraz, Chianti, Cabernet Sauvignon, Valpolicella
Three Cheese and Wild Mushroom Risotto		Merlot, Chianti, Valpolicella
Gnocchi with Gorgonzola and Walnuts		Cabernet Sauvignon, Sangiovese
Gruyère Au Gratin Potatoes	Sauvignon Blanc, Riesling	
Potato Wedges with Sweet Thai Chili Sauce	Gewürztraminer, Riesling	
Cauliflower Au Gratin	Sauvignon Blanc	
Garlic and Gouda Mashed Potatoes	Chardonnay, Riesling, Pinot Gris	
Tunisian Baklawa	Ice wine, Moscato D'Asti	
Mango White Chocolate Crème Brûlée	Moscato D'Asti, Sauternes	
Chocolate Pots de Crème		Port, Muscat
Chocolate Fondue		Port, Muscat, Merlot

Index

From My Travels to Your Table

A Collection of Recipes to DINE For

Norma Jean Will
dba Recipes to DINE For
P.O. Box 4755
Evansville, Indiana 47724-0755
www.recipes2dine4.com

Name

Street Address

City State Zip

Telephone E-mail *(optional)*

Your Order	Qty	Total
From My Travels to Your Table at $24.95 each		$
Indiana residents add 7% sales tax		$
Shipping ($3.95 for one book; $4.95 for two books)		$
Total		$

Method of Payment: [ ] MasterCard [ ] VISA
[ ] Check enclosed payable to Recipes to DINE For

Account Number Expiration Date

Cardholder Name

Signature

Photocopies accepted.